Endless

Possibilities

Exploring the Journeys of

Your Life

by Dr. Lee B. Spitzer

Lincoln, Nebraska

Spiritual Journey Press

Endless Possibilities
Copyright © 1997 by Dr. Lee B. Spitzer

A Spiritual Journey Press Book
First Printing 1997

Queries regarding rights and permissions should be addressed to Spiritual Journey Press, 6536 Rockwood Lane, Lincoln, Nebraska USA 68516-5110. Please write for bulk purchase, church and study group discounts.

For e-mail communications, write to the author at LBSOnline@aol.com.

Scripture taken from the HOLY BIBLE, NEW INTERNATIONAL VERSION®. Copyright© 1973, 1978, 1984 by International Bible Society. Used by permission of Zondervan Publishing House. All rights reserved.

Library of Congress Catalog Card Number: 97-68812
ISBN 1-57502-555-8

Printed in the USA by

MORRIS PUBLISHING
3212 East Highway 30 • Kearney, NE 68847 • 1-800-650-7888

Contents

*Dedicated to
my family,
Lois, Joshua and Larisa.*

*Special thanks to the following people
who contributed to making
this book a reality by offering
their suggestions and feedback:*

*Bruce and Ann Borquist
Rick and Sharon Chatwell
Fred Daugherty
Sandy Denton
Howard and Hazel Keeley
Ann Olson
Bret Rickard
Calvin and Janet Rife
Julie Snyder
Martha Sorenson*

*Thanks also to all of the members of the churches
I have been privileged to serve:*

*Bethlehem Presbyterian Church, Buffalo, New York
St. Mark's Episcopal Church, Glendale, California
Trinity Baptist Church, Lynnfield, Massachusetts
First Baptist Church, East Providence, Rhode Island
Seaview Baptist Church, Linwood, New Jersey
First Baptist Church, Lincoln, Nebraska*

*You have been my teachers
as I have sought
to hear the voice of Jesus,
the Lord of our journeys,
and the source of endless possibilities.*

A Personal Parable

When the chest pains first surfaced on a warm autumn afternoon a number of years ago, I was not particularly concerned. It had been a busy day at church, and I was pleased to have accomplished as much as I did, since I felt a need to make up for taking time off the previous day. In celebration of my wife's birthday, our family spent the afternoon at the Philadelphia Zoo, peering at primates, sneering at slithering snakes, and making faces at ferocious lions and tigers.

The chest pains grew in intensity throughout dinner. By early evening I was finding it difficult to hide my concern, and so feigning tiredness, I excused myself and escaped to my bedroom. Throughout the mostly sleepless night, I charted the location and intensity of the pains, which were sometimes sharp (especially when I moved) and sometimes dull. I just wished that they would disappear.

Throughout the episode, I recalled what parishioners had told me about their heart attack symptoms. Sharp pains radiating from the chest region. The feeling of a huge weight sitting upon one's chest. Shortness of breath. Even though I was only in my early thirties, my personal medical history (I was born with a heart murmur) in conjunction with my family's higher than average heart-related death rate, convinced me to consider the possibility I was experiencing a heart attack, or at least a heart-related problem. After all, my mother had died from a series of heart attacks at age 41, my father succumbed to a heart attack at age 67, and his father passed away at age 27 from this same cause.

When morning arrived and the pains still persisted, I told my wife and Lois promptly arranged for a cardiologist to see me right away. I felt foolish going to him, but rationalized it by assuring myself that since I had not been to a cardiologist for many years, it would be wise to establish a relationship with one once again.

To my surprise, after explaining in detail the symptoms that had led me to his office, he picked up on my casual reference to having visited the zoo the day before the pain manifested itself. Expecting him to do tests and listen pensively to my heart (like the cardiologists from my youth had done on my semi-annual visits), I was taken aback

1

by his greater interest in the zoo experience. He discovered that I had carried a camera bag filled with heavy equipment, and that I had often picked up my two children so that they could have a better view of the caged animals. I sheepishly admitted that I was not the type of person who exercised regularly.

When the cardiologist reached for his prescription pad, I knew the fact finding phase of the visit was over and he had reached a conclusion. As I wondered about whether he was going to send me to the hospital for further tests, he calmly announced that I was not having a heart attack at all, but rather was suffering from pulled muscles around my rib cage. The indicated remedy was the prescription form of Tylenol! Sensing my extreme embarrassment, he politely acknowledged that my symptoms could indicate heart problems, but in my case the context from which they arose in conjunction with his experience as a physician indicated clearly to him that pulled muscles was the preferred diagnosis. And, as time would tell, he was correct.

As I left his office, I wondered why I had not been able to come to the same obvious conclusion. He and I had the same set of facts at our disposal. The difference was that his training as a cardiologist had given him a framework which I did not possess from which to discern the significance of the data and diagnose what was happening to me. His experience and theoretical framework enabled him to ask insightful questions and link the facts of my story together. I did not possess this ability because I lacked knowledge of the framework and had not been trained to apply it to my life experience.

Most people have a difficult time diagnosing their spiritual experiences and placing them within a coherent framework. How do we discern what is significant in our spiritual experience? How do we connect the dots between the discrete events of life? How do we extrapolate meaning from the spiritual encounters we seek with God? How do we communicate those encounters in a way that avoids tired clichés? Can we be trained in seeing the underlying patterns which represent God's will for our journeys? How do we discover God's will? Are there doctors "of the soul" who can diagnose and recommend remedies for what ails our spirits? For all those who have asked these or similar questions, this book represents good news - the answer is "Yes!"

Chapter One

What Is A Spiritual Journey?

Searching for a Meaningful Life

For life to be meaningful, reflective people search for themes and patterns which integrate seemingly unrelated life experiences into a coherent whole. We intuitively seek "an explanation of it all" even in times when scientific rationalism strives to ignore the spiritual mystery that people continually rediscover. We need to know why experiences come our way, and we wish to believe that there is an underlying rationality or purpose to the course of our lives.

Our Christian faith welcomes and validates this search, and asserts that there are two levels of order that are to be found in the structure of creation. First, there is *truth*. In Christ there can be found ultimate truth concerning our salvation and reconciliation with God, sound theology, and ethics and morality. This doctrinal level of order is foundational to one's own faith perspective and practice.

Second, the Bible affirms that God also has control over the events and course of human history, as Jeremiah says, "'For I know the plans that I have for you,' declares the LORD, 'plans for welfare and not for calamity to give you a future and a hope'" (Jeremiah 29:11). If God has a plan for our lives, then it is reasonable to assert that He will arrange and structure our life experiences to enable us to achieve His goals and aims.

The discovery of a plan weaving its way through one's life inevitably encourages a person to formulate a *story* - an intensely personal perspective on how one's own journey expresses coherence and meaning: "Stories are crucial because they communicate to a person both an identity and a vision of the world . . . Stories help make sense of the world; they take apparently disconnected bits and pieces and show how they fit together into a whole."[1]

This holds true for both individuals and societies. Groups of people, as well as individuals, express their identity and vision of the world through the telling of stories. Within a Christian context, this insight reminds Christians that we are people who celebrate the story of God's redeeming work within history through Christ, and that as a result, individual believers and church groups have significant stories of their own to appreciate, live out, and share with others.

As leaders of churches, pastors are entrusted with the task of *spiritual direction*, the ministry of helping individual people and groups to articulate how God's presence and grace (in all of its various manifestations) enter into their lives and thus, their stories. The aim of spiritual direction is to invite people to respond with faith and commitment to this provision of divine grace (which is the work of the Holy Spirit). Faith and commitment, however, must be accompanied by understanding and wisdom, for faith without understanding is often little more than blind emotionalism, and commitment without wisdom breeds an ignorant fanaticism that scarcely can be said to resemble a Biblical response to life's complexities, challenges and responsibilities.

We Need a Spiritual Journey Paradigm

The fruit of sound understanding and wisdom is a *spiritual journey paradigm* - a world-view or perspective that expresses the coherence of our individual and collective ongoing spiritual experience. A paradigm is a model (an abstract distillation) of the significant patterns that reappear in our personal and communal stories, providing us with a common language with which to communicate our particular spiritual journey experiences to one another.

For the Christian, this world-view must be in accord with Biblical revelation. There are a number of general principles which we must keep in mind as we seek to develop a Biblical model or paradigm of spiritual journeying.

First, *a spiritual journey results from God's interaction with human beings through time.* Spiritual journeys emerge from the intention of God for our lives and are embraced by us as we intentionally or unconsciously respond to both the divine initiative and historical circumstances. This spiritual dance cannot be reduced to a finite number of isolated and unrelated divine/human encounters, for then we could not speak of journeys but only of events. Each discrete experience of God is part of a process which transcends any individual moment, and thus it may only be understood and appreciated if we look at it from the perspective of its place within the journey.

Second, *a spiritual journey may be explained by identifying and describing its phases or stages.* Spiritual journeys are not haphazard or purposeless experiences. Most human activities evidence, upon reflection, a pattern which can be used either to repeat an activity or to explain how a person journeys from point A to B.

Stage or phase language, when applied to spiritual journeys, provides us with an objective way of relating spiritual experience so that others may relate their experiences to ours even when the specific details of the experience may differ. For example, a vacation trip usually involves these stages: planning where to go, packing, getting there, having fun at the destination, and returning home. This holds true whether one goes camping in the Rockies or spends a week in Disneyworld. Spiritual journey stage language can be overlayed on our particular experience so that patterns may emerge which give us insight into how God is working in and through our lives.

Third, *a spiritual journey paradigm assists us in understanding the significance of our spiritual experiences.* Spiritual journeys are integral to human existence and as such provide human life with its meaningfulness. Spiritual journey paradigms provide the framework from which we explore the value and essence of our journeys. Since different paradigms will explain the same journey in different ways, it is vital that we consciously assess the paradigms we have either inherited or adopted. It should be emphasized at this point that spiritual journey paradigms are not synonymous with the Gospel or with a received body of doctrinal truth, but instead describe observed patterns of human responses to the Gospel and life in general.

Fourth, *a comprehensive spiritual journey paradigm balances inner spiritual growth with other-centered service.* In a world which so short-sightedly worships celebrity and skill over character and personal integrity, we must be reminded that this life affords us with an opportunity to respond to God's grace by embracing virtues and forsaking sin. Similarly, we must reject the modern desire for instant gratification by affirming that human wholeness and maturation takes time and must proceed according to stages.

Furthermore, a spiritual journey paradigm reminds us of our call to serve others. An authentic spiritual journey theology should lead us beyond a narcissistic concern for ourselves so that our talents, gifts and skills can be employed for the sake of humanity and the rest of creation. Above all, a spiritual journey paradigm must clearly remind us that the central task of humanity (both on an individual and corporate basis) is to respond to God's call by fulfilling His will. Fulfilling God's will is what spiritual journeying is all about.

As people who are committed to journeying as a means of fulfilling God's will, Christians should understand their stories and communicate them in ways that are relevant to contemporary society, faithful to reality, expressive of the truths of the Biblical revelation, and existentially meaningful. We need a spiritual journey paradigm!

Goal-Oriented Journeying as a Central Motif of The Spiritual Life

Goal-oriented journeying is a Biblical motif which helps us understand how God orders our lives. Sandwiched in between two depictions of perfection (the Garden of Eden before humanity's fall and the New Jerusalem in which sinless perfection has been restored) are the Biblical accounts of God's people journeying in response to God's call towards a goal or destination even though they live in a world fractured by sin.

Abraham leaves his homeland in order to discover the promised land. Joseph journeys to Egypt (unwillingly, to be sure) and is used by God to save his family and the Egyptians during a time of famine. Moses leads Israel from Egypt to Canaan on a journey of liberation that lasted more than forty years. This journey embodied the central theme of Israel's religious experience, and its lessons were ingrained into the hearts and minds of each succeeding generation of Jews.

The chronicles of the judges, prophets and kings of later Old Testament history also are illustrative of the goal-oriented journeying motif. The book of Judges depicts the individual goal-oriented journeys of leaders such as Deborah, Gideon, and Samson in light of the downward spiral of Israel's corporate spiritual journey. David's legendary journeys are recounted in both the historical and poetic sections of the Old Testament. In the post-exilic era, Nehemiah and Ezra journey with God's people from captivity back to Judah. And perhaps the most well-known Old Testament story - that of Jonah and the sea creature - describes that reluctant prophet's spiritual journey away from and then back toward the ministry goals that God had ordained for him.

In the New Testament, the journeying motif remains central. John the Baptist journeys throughout Israel in order to set the stage for Jesus' messianic ministry. Jesus Himself is depicted in all four Gospels as an itinerant teacher, who spends his whole ministry journeying from one town to another, with Jerusalem as his ultimate destination and the Cross as his spiritual goal. Jesus teaches his disciples by allowing them to accompany him on his journeys, and by sending them on their own short-term journeys to practice what they had observed.

Paul's Christian experience begins while he is on a journey, and his subsequent life and ministry can easily be recounted as a series of personal and apostolic ministry journeys. Peter's ministry takes him from Jerusalem to Rome, and John's journey brings him to Patmos, where he records visions of the Messiah's return journey back to our world and the Church's journey through tribulation and into eternity.

Accordingly, goal-oriented journeying should be considered a central motif for the Christian life. Conversion is portrayed as a transfer or journey from one kingdom into another (Colossians 1:13). In Philippians, Paul characterizes the movement of the Christian life by saying that he "presses on" towards God's goal for his life. He is particularly fond of expressing the flow of Christian life by employing the "walking" metaphor. To the Philippians, he says that those who follow him should "walk according to the pattern you have in us" (Philippians 3:12-17). Consider also these passages:

I, therefore, the prisoner of the Lord, entreat you to walk in a manner worthy of the calling with which you have been called. (Ephesians 4:1)

Finally then, brethren, we request and exhort you in the Lord Jesus, that, as you received from us instruction as to how you ought to walk and please God (just as you actually do walk), that you may excel still more. (1 Thessalonians 4:1)

7

Both Paul and the writer to the Hebrews conceive of the Christian life as a race that must be run by Jesus' disciples:

> Do you not know that those who run in a race all run, but only one receives the prize? Run in such a way that you may win . . . Therefore, I run in such a way, as not without aim. . . (1 Corinthians 9:24, 26a)

> Therefore, since we have so great a cloud of witnesses surrounding us, let us also lay aside every encumbrance, and the sin which so easily entangles us, and let us run with endurance the race that is set before us, fixing our eyes on Jesus, the author and perfecter of faith, who for the joy set before Him endured the cross, despising the shame, and has sat down at the right hand of the throne of God. (Hebrews 12:1-2)

Regardless of whether the motion of the Christian life is described as walking or running a race, the underlying emphasis remains the same: Christians are called to be people on the move. This movement is not aimless, but rather purposeful as we discover, embrace and fulfill the will of God for our lives by realizing the goals He has determined for our journeys.

Discovering the Patterns of Our Goal-Oriented Spiritual Journeys

Having embraced goal-oriented journeying as a key metaphor of the Christian's spiritual journey experience, we next take up the task of discerning if spiritual journeys follow certain recurring patterns. Such patterns do not exist in relation to the *content* of our journeys. The particular goals that animate my life (the specific vision for my ministry, for example) do not apply to other people who feel an equally valid call to ministry or to serving God.

However, on a *phenomenological* (experiential) level, significant patterns do emerge as we analyze the spiritual journeys of both Biblical and contemporary pilgrims. These patterns provide the basic outline of the Goal-Oriented Spiritual Journey Paradigm that informs my ministry as a spiritual director and that has so richly increased my understanding of my own personal spiritual journey experiences.

8

Stated simply, *Christians pass through five distinct phases in each journey they embrace in response to God's call.* These five phases describe how we are guided by God to achieve His purposes throughout our lives.

Phase One: The Unconscious Journey

(Preparation)

My conversion to the Christian faith took me by surprise and was not anticipated by anyone who knew me. I had not shown any interest in Christianity, and in fact despised Christians in particular and Gentiles in general because of the travesty of the Holocaust and other manifestations of anti-Semitism which littered history.

Nevertheless, at the age of fourteen, I embraced Jesus Christ as my "Messiah and Master" through an unexpected and unsought mystical experience, and converted from Judaism, the faith of my family for millennia.

It did not take me long after that conversion experience to notice that in hindsight, there were many indications that God had prepared me for that decisive faith commitment. Religiously speaking, what better preparation can there be for Christian faith than a Jewish background? As a child, I loved the Old Testament, especially holding dear the prophetic hope of a messianic age which would bring shalom to the world.

From the age of seven, I had experienced a recurring dream which I kept secret. I was in Israel on a mountain, pointing to a powerful and holy rider on a white horse coming down from the heavens, and saying, "There is my Messiah!" On the night of my conversion, God led me to read the concluding pages of the New Testament, only to discover my dream in written form in Revelation 19:11-21! This was the first time I had ever read the New Testament.

My Jewish heritage also stressed the need for repentance and forgiveness when God's laws are broken, as symbolized by such holy observances as Passover and Yom Kippur. Raised with high expectations for my future as a scholar, I internalized a perfectionist outlook which caused me to be highly critical of any mistakes,

9

especially those I could have avoided. I took no solace in contemporary Judaism's symbolic sin offerings, yearning instead for the kind of sacrifice spoken of in the Torah - a substitutionary atonement which would grant me reconciliation with the God of Abraham, Isaac, Jacob, and Moses.

My dreams would be realized when I turned from Revelation to the first page of the New Testament. The opening genealogy of Matthew may bore most people, but it contained a revelation to me - like me, Jesus Christ was Jewish (I had always categorized him as a Christian leader). But what really rocked my soul was the angelic pronouncement that Jesus would "save his people from their sins" (Matthew 1:21). "His people" were the Jews - my people - and if he came to save them, he had come to save me from my perfectionist ordeal. The Messiah on the white horse was none other than Jesus, whom I had grown up despising! And he had come for me, on a wintry night in 1971, calling me to journey as a faithful follower. My past was a prelude for the future.

One of the most fascinating aspects of the spiritual life is the realization that we begin heading towards a goal long before we discover what the goal actually is or even that the journey has begun. In this phase, *we pack for the trip* by picking up skills, tools and insights that will become invaluable later on when we discover how God intends to put them to use. This process of *packing* is often not the result of a conscious choice on our part, but simply is the work of God within us so that we will be prepared for the demands and challenges of the future.

Examples of the unconscious phase of the spiritual journey abound in Scripture:

- *Joseph* is given the opportunity to hear from God in dreams as a youth, and this sets in motion a whole series of events which enable him to rise to the highest levels of power in Egypt and so save the people (and his own family) from famine and starvation.

- *Esther*, through a beauty contest, becomes the Queen of Persia, and finds herself in a position to use her beauty, charm

10

and craftiness to save the Jews from annihilation. She did not choose this journey, but God did, and behind the scenes He manipulated events so that His ends might be achieved.

- *Saul of Tarsus* is led by God as a youth to delve deeply into the wisdom of Judaism so that he will be able to articulate the intricacies of the New Covenant in an authoritative way.

- *Luke*, a physician by training, discovers later on in his life that the skills he learned for this profession equip him beautifully to complement Paul's apostolic ministry and to write Luke-Acts for the first-century church.

Phase one is an existential experience or personal realization of the doctrines of grace and predestination. This phase of the journey is wholly dependent on God's willingness to fashion our lives according to His vision of the future. He must initiate the process for it to be fruitful, and its fruitfulness is conditioned on God's ability to see what is precisely needed in our futures.

God does not begin a process in our lives by chance or on a whim, but rather because He has specific and achievable goals in mind for the course of our lives on this globe. When Jeremiah receives his call to the prophetic ministry, he is assured that God was preparing him for this special goal-oriented journey long before he became aware of it: "The word of the LORD came to me, saying, 'Before I formed you in the womb I knew you, before you were born I set you apart; I appointed you as a prophet to the nations'" (Jeremiah 1:4-5). According to Paul, Jeremiah was not the only one for whom God has ever prepared a journey:

> Praise be to the God and Father of our Lord Jesus Christ, who has blessed us in the heavenly realms with every spiritual blessing in Christ. For he chose us in him before the creation of the world to be holy and blameless in his sight. In love he predestined us to be adopted as his sons through Jesus Christ, in accordance with his pleasure and will - to the praise of his glorious grace, which he has freely given us in the One He loves. (Ephesians 1:3-6)

It is vitally important to recognize that the initiation of the journey is not dependent on us or our actions, but rather on God's working out

11

of His desires for our lives. Any other understanding of the process will inevitably lead to self-aggrandizement instead of the glorification of God in our lives. Thus, John makes it clear that the love we possess is the result of what God initiated in our lives: "We love because he first loved us" (1 John 4:19). The spiritual journey, then, is a gift from God which He initiates with a view towards achieving the goals He has set for our lives (Ephesians 2:8-10).

Since the journey is initiated by God and is not dependent on our conscious assent or cooperation, phase one can best be described psychologically as an *unconscious journey*. It can only be comprehended fully in hindsight, and not while it is occurring. The unconscious journey represents God's willingness to prepare us for the spiritual task to which we feel called, and thus we can affirm that our very sense of call has its roots in God's actions on our behalf.

Phase Two: The Encounter with Revelation

(Discovery)

Three years after my discovery that Jesus was my Messiah, God revealed another surprise that would change my life's course. Halfway through my senior year in high school, I was eagerly awaiting acceptance letters from a half-dozen universities, most of them Ivy League. The time had come to embark on my pre-law degree, a necessary stepping stone toward my dream of becoming a constitutional lawyer. I couldn't think of a better way to serve God than by devoting my life to issues of social justice.

During a personal prayer time, the Lord unexpectedly spoke to my heart about His plans for my future. He clearly stated that after I received my acceptance letters in April, I should decline the invitation to attend those colleges because He was going to send me elsewhere. And instead of training for practicing law, I should prepare to be a pastor!

I laughed out loud due to shock, and urged God to reconsider. I reminded Him of the value of practicing law, of my aptitude for the discipline, and of the significant fact that I did not belong to any church. This last fact should certainly disqualify me from being a minister, I politely but insistently concluded.

God apparently was not impressed with my arguments. An interior voice firmly reminded me that there was no justice issue I could not address as a minister, that the same skills are required for both vocations, and that I had been leading a Bible study for a group of young people for almost three years in which I had demonstrated ministerial gifts. As for going to church, I would be involved with one shortly!

For more than a month, I secretly wrestled with God over this issue. During that whole time, I felt no peace while I tried to reconcile my devotion to God with my personal aspirations. By the middle of January, 1975, my struggle came to a conclusion. I decided to say "yes" to God's call, began participating in a church, and started seeking God's will concerning what Christian college to attend. My journey as a minister of Jesus Christ was underway!

Phase two marks the beginning of our conscious participation in the spiritual journey. In this phase, we are confronted with the unveiling of God's plan for a particular part of our lives. Specifically, we *discover* the task-specific goal or purpose for our journey, and (usually to our surprise) we look back at the events of phase one and realize for the first time the significance of certain events which have transpired. Our past takes on new meaning when we see the future more clearly. Seemingly isolated events and personal relationships now share a connectedness that had been hidden from us as we travelled through the unconscious phase of our journey. Thus, this phase produces a sense of excitement for us as we say "Aha!" to ourselves and to God.[2]

Furthermore, phase two involves a spiritual awakening and the reception of new insights which have the potential of totally changing the way we view the world and our role in it. It is analogous to a conversion experience, since conversion is "not a cop-out, not cotton batting to protect us from life, but a discovery of a new force, a new person, a new center in life that makes us eager to meet new challenges and to be relevant in the affairs of men."[3]

13

By framing the phase two experience as a salvation-like discovery of the grace of God which re-orients us to new purposes, we are asserting that this discovery is also a summons to journey towards a goal. We tend to picture salvation as bringing benefits to a person such as forgiveness of sins, eternal life, God's unconditional love and acceptance - and rightly so. Yet salvation is more than the reception of a divine package of presents. It also involves the divine call to journey, under the Lordship of Jesus, towards God's will. In arguing that the church is not a "commissary" (the dispenser of religious goods and services), but rather a "caravan" (a people on the move), Vernard Eller asserts:

> Throughout the Old Testament (and rather prominently in the New) we see that the archetype of salvation is the Passover and the exodus event. If that be so, then it is plain that salvation cannot be understood as a state of having it made, of settling down to enjoy a condition of secure accomplishment. Instead, salvation is the experience of being made free to travel, of being called out by a leader-lord and enabled to follow him on his way to the kingdom.[4]

Paul's journey to Damascus is an impressive example of the impact that phase two can have on a person. Paul travels toward Damascus in order to persecute the church (or so he believes), but in reality God has set him on that journey for an entirely different reason. This is revealed to Paul after he sets out and encounters a revelation of Christ's presence (Acts 9:1-8). As an integral part of this revelation, Paul discovers who Christ is and what his new mission in life is to be. Before Agrippa, Paul interpreted this moment of revelation in the following way:

> Then I said, "Who art Thou, Lord?" And the Lord said, "I am Jesus whom you are persecuting. But arise, and stand on your feet; for this purpose I have appeared to you, to appoint you a minister and a witness not only to the things which you have seen, but also to the things in which I will appear to you; delivering you from the Jewish people and from the Gentiles, to whom I am sending you, to open their eyes so that they may turn from darkness to light and from the dominion of Satan to God, in order that they may receive forgiveness of sins and an inheritance

among those who have been sanctified by faith in Me." (Acts 26:15-18)

Not only does God reveal a journey goal as we discover our calling, but He also usually provides us with the knowledge of who is going to be affected by the journey and its goals. Paul is informed that his apostolic ministry will be primarily to the Gentiles of the Roman Empire who have not heard the Gospel. Jonah is given a message of judgment and an intended audience, the people of Nineveh. Moses is called to deliver the Jews from Pharaoh's harsh rule.

There is no experiential or Biblical norm by which such a revelation must be experienced. It may be captured by a peak religious experience such as a vision or a religiously significant dream, by a flash of insight that puts everything in a new light for us, or through a quiet but progressive unveiling that is not accompanied by any spectacular outward manifestation. The mode that is selected by God for the unveiling of His plan is not in and of itself significant; all that matters is that the revelation has been received, understood and accepted by us.

Phase two is brought to a completion when we consciously own the revelation's call by embracing it. The call demands a response on our part, and the response for which God is searching is our willingness and commitment to travel towards the journey's goal. It also affords us an opportunity to manifest obedience, as Paul's recounting of his own revelation illustrates:

"Consequently, King Agrippa, I did not prove disobedient to the heavenly vision, but kept declaring both to those of Damascus first, and also at Jerusalem and then throughout all the region of Judea, and even to the Gentiles, that they should repent and turn to God, performing deeds appropriate to repentance." (Acts 26:19-20)

All of the major characteristics of the phase two discovery of a summons to embrace a spiritual journey can be found in Isaiah's call to be a prophet (Isaiah 6:1-13). Isaiah encounters the presence of God (in this instance, in a mystical experience), and becomes aware of and confesses his own imperfection (vv. 1-5). After receiving absolution, he hears the call to fulfill a goal-oriented journey and embraces it. He is to preach a message of holiness and repentance to Israel, who will

15

not be receptive (vv. 6-10). Although no specific timetable is given for the duration of the journey, the circumstances surrounding the journey's conclusion are generally described (vv. 11-13). God rarely reveals a journey's duration during this phase; Jeremiah's prophecy concerning Israel's seventy year exile (Jeremiah 25:12-14) is a noteworthy exception. A New Testament example of God's reticence in this regard is Jesus' refusal in Acts 1:6-7 to reveal when the church's Great Commission journey will be over.

Phase Three: The Conscious Journey
(Cooperation)

Having turned down Harvard, Yale, Princeton and a number of other prestigious schools, I began my college experience at a small Christian liberal arts school in New York, The King's College. Sensing that God had called me not only to take courses, but also to serve him by practicing ministerial skills, I began a nightly student prayer and Bible study meeting.

On the first night, the only other person at the meeting was my best friend, Lois, a young Jewish woman from my hometown who had previously converted to Christ through the influence of my high school Bible study. On the second night, two other women joined us. By the end of the first semester, the group regularly attracted twenty students and was one of the few activities that was fully inter-racial in character at the school.

Most of the group also felt led to support evangelism efforts, ministering to people at a Christian coffeehouse in Greenwich Village, and pioneering evangelistic book tables in New York City's Penn Station, Port Authority Bus Terminal and Central Park. By pooling our spiritual gifts together, this remarkable group of young people grew in maturity and in service, changing lives in the process.

Years later, during my first pastorate in Rhode Island, a handful of members of American Baptist churches from around the state decided that God wanted us to witness about our faith by promoting a gospel of peace and social justice. We created a new organization, the American Baptist Peacemakers of Rhode Island, which I had the privilege of serving as president. Instead of creating committees which regularly had to meet even if there was no business at hand, we organized task forces which were designed to reach a specific goal and would cease when the goal was met. Members of the task force were not selected by a representational system (which often puts people on committees who are not dedicated to fulfilling the group's task) but by assigning people on the basis of their sense of call and possession of appropriate spiritual gifts.

As a result, this vibrant group achieved far more than our numbers suggested were possible. We lobbied Congress on bills, sponsored public meetings, produced an Advent devotional on peacemaking, sent representatives on international peace missions, and reminded our congregations of the necessity of living out our faith by struggling for societal justice.

Phase two, the encounter with revelation, provides us with the goal we need to bring direction to our spiritual journeys. In phase three, God enlists our active and intentional participation towards a goal-related end, based upon our commitment to serve Him and others in submission to His will.

To pick up the journeying analogy once more, if phase one represents the packing for a trip and phase two involves finding out our destination, then phase three is characterized by actually getting into the car and *traveling towards the destination.* It is a time when knowledge becomes wedded with action and when conviction leads to concrete application. It is a time when God calls for our active and conscious *cooperation* in manifesting one aspect of His vision of the kingdom of God. Paul sums up the dynamics of this phase when he writes:

I want to know Christ and the power of his resurrection and the fellowship of sharing in his sufferings, becoming like him in his death, and so, somehow, to attain to the resurrection from the dead. Not that I have already obtained all this, or have already been made perfect, but I press on to take hold of that for which Christ Jesus took hold of me. Brothers, I do not consider myself yet to have taken hold of it. But one thing I do: Forgetting what is behind and straining toward what is ahead, I press on toward the goal to win the prize for which God has called me heavenward in Christ Jesus." (Philippians 3:10-14)

The use of the term *cooperation* to describe the relational interaction during phase three demands clarification. In this context, *cooperation* denotes *the Christian's conscious experience of God and His people working together toward a common task-specific spiritual journey goal.* An example of this is Acts 5:32, where the disciples and the Holy Spirit are co-witnesses of the Gospel; both have a part to play in sharing the good news of Jesus Christ. In 2 Corinthians 6:1, Paul affirms that his apostolic ministry involves cooperating or "working together" with God in the spreading of the Gospel.[5]

Under no circumstances should the employment of the term *cooperation* in this context be construed as implying that humans cooperate with God in securing their own salvation, just as Paul's admonition to the Philippians "to work out their salvation" (Philippians 2:12) does not mean that it is possible to gain salvation through good works. Rather, the use of *cooperation* in this context is akin to the Pauline observation that in Christian experience we sense that "it is God who is at work in you, both to will and to work for His good pleasure" (Philippians 2:13).

Furthermore, the use of *cooperation* to designate the perception of God's empowering presence as one works towards a goal should not be interpreted as placing God and the pilgrim on an equal footing. God *always* "cooperates" as Lord within the relationship, and humanity always as servant.[6]

We must embark on the conscious phase of the spiritual journey with a strong desire to reach the goal that God has set for us. A pilgrim without motivation and enthusiasm will be easily discouraged by the eventual opposition and roadblocks that hinder progress. The conscious phase of the spiritual journey involves not only ministry and vocational successes, but also necessarily those experiences of the "fellowship of sharing in his sufferings" (Philippians 3:10).

Theologically, phase three of the spiritual journey corresponds to the sanctification of the believer in Christ and his or her empowerment for mission by the Holy Spirit. It is the outworking of the calling to be a disciple even as the process of sanctification is the inevitable result of responding to the call of salvation. When Paul writes to the

18

Philippians that they should "work out your salvation with fear and trembling, for it is God who works in you to will and to act according to his good purpose" (Philippians 2:12-13), the Christian hears the call to take responsibility for his or her spiritual journey and to manifest the reality of true faith by producing the appropriate good works, with the necessary and sufficient aid of God's power.

If the encounter with revelation sets the stage for the conscious journey, then our being empowered or anointed with the Holy Spirit is essential for us as we begin to venture towards our goal. Accordingly, Jesus instructs His disciples to remain at their home base in Jerusalem until after they have personally experienced an influx of the power of the Spirit for ministry (Luke 24:48-49). Jesus Himself did not begin his ministry until the Holy Spirit fell upon Him at His baptism (Matthew 3:16-17; Luke 3:21-22; 4:14-21).

The power of the Spirit will not only be manifested through miracles and the appearance of the various gifts of the Spirit (Acts 2:1-12; 1 Corinthians 12:1-11; Hebrews 2:4), but also through the equally important authenticating assurance that the Spirit gives as we share the words of truth and justice (Micah 3:8; Acts 5:32). Such interaction between the Spirit and the believer exemplifies just how close the cooperation between God and the Christian needs to be during the conscious journey phase.

Phase Four: Reaching the Goal

(Arrival)

Saying good-bye to a church produces some of the richest moments in a pastor's life.

I remember Linda, a teenager from the youth group at an Episcopal church I served during my seminary years, running from me during my farewell party because she didn't want to see me leave. When we finally did say our good-byes a few days later, grieving together, peace came to both of us.

I cherished the opportunity to be one of the speakers at my mentor's farewell worship service and party at Trinity Baptist Church in Lynnfield, Massachusetts. Speaking on behalf of the many

seminary students who had profited by Howard Keeley's supervision,
I reviewed how God had used this special man to inspire a church to
take extraordinary risks during his sixteen year journey as the
church's pastor. I joked that my remarks could double as a funeral
message, and the congregation's mixture of laughter and tears
confirmed that this good-bye felt like a grief experience.

I recall my visit to Gertrude, one of my favorite elderly members
of First Baptist Church in East Providence, Rhode Island. I didn't
want her to find out about my resignation from the letter I had placed
in the mail, and so I invited myself over to her house. I've never
forgotten her reaction to my announcement that the others would
receive the next day. She declared, "Pastor, by tomorrow you'll be
nothing but a memory!"

The call to complete the conscious journey does not envision the
specific goal as an end in itself, but rather as a way in which to draw
closer to Christ. Everything that is done in life finds its ultimate
meaning only in so far as it helps us to redefine and enhance our
relationship with God. The most grave temptation open to the
Christian is to allow one's agenda to gain the status of the most
important thing in life, with everything and everyone else becoming
subordinate to it. Self-fulfillment must not become our idol. We do
not grow closer to God in order to reach our goals, for this is
tantamount to using or manipulating God for personal ends. Rather,
we understand that journeying toward goals facilitates our quest to
grow closer to God.

The most important activities of phase four are *reflection* and
worship. Of course, we should engage in both exercises throughout
every phase of our journeys, but they represent the very essence of
phase four.

Through reflection, we review the journeying process in order to
discover how God interacted with us during the course of our journey.
Arriving at our destination enables us to gain perspective on the trials
and triumphs that we experienced (Revelation 7:9-17). It is not
sufficient simply to experience events without reflection; we must also
gain insight into their meaning in order to truly complete the journey
and enjoy its wisdom.

Reflection and self-discovery draw us into a spirit of worship. The most appropriate response to discovering the changes that have taken place within and through us is to worship God. And as we worship and discover that "from Him and through Him and to Him are all things" (Romans 11:36), we affirm that the reward of one's spiritual journey is to become united with God in His love.

In many ways, phase four of our goal-oriented spiritual journeys is analogous to what we experience at the conclusion of our lives. Paul's assessment of his own personal spiritual journey toward the end of his life is representative of what every mature Christian feels at the conclusion of a goal-oriented journey which has been faithfully embraced and completed: "I have fought the good fight, I have finished the course, I have kept the faith" (2 Timothy 4:7).

Reaching the conclusion of a goal-oriented spiritual journey involves a kind of death experience. Of course, we do not die physically every time we conclude a short-term goal-oriented spiritual journey. Instead, we experience death-like *surrogate experiences*, such as a sense of loss, despair, grief or depression after our goal has been reached. Often this is referred to as "the letdown" that hits us after the completion of a significant experience.

The idea that reaching the goal is a death experience is literally fulfilled in Jesus' messianic goal-oriented spiritual journey. Jesus equates his sacrificial death with the reaching of his journey's goal (John 12:23-33):

> Just at that time some Pharisees came up, saying to Him, "Go away and depart from here, for Herod wants to kill you." And he said to them, "Go and tell that fox, 'Behold, I cast out demons and perform cures today and tomorrow, and the third day I reach my goal.' Nevertheless, I must journey on today and tomorrow and the next day; for it cannot be that a prophet should perish outside of Jerusalem." (Luke 13:31-33)

A phase four death experience is not the end of our spiritual lives any more than Jesus' death ended His journey or life. It is instead a profoundly deep and mysterious transition to a new realization of the life-giving power of God. Jesus declares that "unless a grain of wheat falls into the earth and dies, it remains by itself alone; but if it dies, it bears much fruit" (John 12:24). His death, at the end of His

21

goal-oriented journey as the Messiah of Israel, releases the resurrection power that brings life to us all.

Similarly, the conclusions of our goal-oriented spiritual journeys do not signal the onset of some impenetrable barrier of dismal finality, but rather the opportunity to identify with Jesus' passage from life, through death, to resurrection. Alan Jones writes: "It's as if death is necessary for the release of new energy. That is why death was often conceived of in sacrificial terms. It was the means by which life was made new."[7]

It also turns out that death (both in its literal and surrogate manifestations) is the means by which goal-oriented spiritual journeys are made new.

Phase Five: Resurrection and New Life
(Renewal)

When I left Rhode Island to accept a call to be the pastor of the Seaview Baptist Church in Linwood, New Jersey, I honestly grieved most over saying good-bye to my association with the peacemaking group I had helped to found. My grief over leaving my church was offset by the joyous anticipation of serving a new one, but I had no corresponding anticipation in regard to my social justice ministry. In fact, God had indicated to me that my active participation in the anti-nuclear movement had come to an end.

During those initial years in New Jersey, we discerned that my son had developmental disabilities, necessitating visits at a local out-patient clinic sponsored by a hospital for children. After my son graduated from its program, a church member (the former mayor of one of the neighboring municipalities) asked me for a favor. He had learned that the hospital was going to merge with a hospital in Philadelphia, and that the out-patient clinic was in danger of being closed, leaving no resource for area children. He wanted me to attend a meeting with the area health care systems agency to protest the merger.

Little did I realize that his invitation would lead me on a ministry journey which would give back to me the purpose and joy I felt when

22

I was involved in the peace movement. By the end of that health systems meeting, I was appointed the chairperson of a fact finding board and with the mayor's daughter, became the co-leader of a people's protest movement. We fought for a new out-patient clinic and held up the merger until the hospitals agreed to serve the children of our region. It was a journey worth waiting for!

After we have reached the goal of each spiritual journey during this life, we experience a kind of spiritual resurrection and new life. From a spiritual journey perspective, resurrection and new life are experienced whenever God begins the call to a new and different journey. When the letdown of the phase four death experience is replaced by a new sense of vitality and purpose, we feel like new people. Once this has occurred, we are already well on our way along a new unconscious journey (phase one) that will lead us into the future.

Paul looks forward to phase five of his apostolic ministry journey when he writes these words to Timothy: "in the future there is laid up for me the crown of righteousness, which the Lord, the righteous Judge, will award to me on that day; and not only to me, but also to all who have loved His appearing" (2 Timothy 4:8). Paul anticipates not only his death, but also his resurrection and the granting of new life.

Although phases one and five both describe "unconscious" or preparatory journey experiences, this does not imply a spiritual or historical circularity or repetition (as, for example, is the case in Hindu and Buddhist views of the spiritual life). Quite the opposite is in fact the case, since the person who experiences phase five is not the exact same person who had earlier traveled through phase one. In the interim period, spiritual growth has occurred, and thus it is a more mature, experienced and aware person who enters into the final phase of the journey.

Furthermore, each goal-oriented spiritual journey is unique and non-repeatable. Every new spiritual journey is built upon the foundation of all the journeys that preceded it and thus takes us beyond them to new goals and life experiences. Accordingly, the Biblical goal-oriented spiritual journey is better represented by a *spiral* than a closed circle.

The Spiral Nature of Our Journeys

The spiral image is also to be preferred over a simplistic use of linearity when we chart goal-oriented spiritual journeys, even though the Judeo-Christian concept of history is often symbolized by the use of a straight line, pointing from the Garden of Eden to the second coming and God's judgment. The course of human history is indeed purposeful and will in the future come to a glorious climax.

Yet our experience of the flow of history in our lives is that the best path from one point to another is often not a straight line, but rather a curved (and sometimes even a rather jagged) one. Anyone who has ever examined the path jets cover as they wing across our globe knows this to be true.

The spiral represents the fact that our journeys and lives do not usually progress in a linear fashion, but instead encounter unexpected curves and turns which seem to take us off course. Through the providential hand of God, it turns out that those supposed detours guide us right to the destinations for which we set out originally, bringing with them unanticipated benefits. Only the misguided and impatient demand a simple linear sojourn through life; experienced travellers realize that the best part of any trip consists of exploring the byways which hold so many surprises and treasures. A spiral notion of spiritual journeying preserves the linear model's constructive emphasis on progress (as opposed to a circular model of the significance of history), while also preserving the complexity and unpredictability of life.

The spiral model also possesses other advantages as a way of envisioning the course of our goal-oriented journeys. While circular models mistakenly diminish the unique significance of past, present and future by relativizing them (no point on a circle is more important than any other point), a simplistic straight-line or linear model may fall into the trap of emphasizing the future to such an extent that the past is denied its due importance.

The spiral pattern, in contrast, seeks to give both the past and future their rightful place. Whether visualized as a two-dimensional or a three-dimensional picture, the space allotted to the beginning of the spiral is less than the ending. As our goal-oriented journeys progress towards the fulfillment of God's will, we grow in wisdom, understanding, faithfulness, and life experience. Through our goal-oriented spiritual journeys, we become more than we were by the grace of God. Also, the flow of the spiral is always from inward to outward, from the past, through the present, towards the future. The spiral affirms that the goal of the journey is to be found in the future, and so that's the direction we must travel.

The spiral imagery values the past, not only by recognizing that it is the source of the journey, but also by suggesting that the future is best approached by periodically and creatively reflecting upon our pasts (a major project of phase four). As we gain a progressively deeper awareness and appreciation of the nature, purpose, meaning, significance and evolution of our spiralling spiritual journeys, we also will sense how privileged we are to be participants in those adventures. If this awareness and appreciation is authentic, we will also welcome a correspondingly deeper sense of personal commitment to the journeys and responsibility for living them out faithfully.[8]

Chapter Two

Goal-Oriented Spiritual Journeying

Does the Bible Teach Goal-Oriented Spiritual Journeying?

Goal-oriented spiritual journeying is solidly supported by the Biblical witness. The paradigm is an analysis of the life stories of men and women whose spiritual journeys are recorded in the Scriptures. The patterns that emerge from this examination may be accepted as a valid teaching of Scripture concerning the course of human experience.

When Paul cites the Exodus experience of Israel, he declares that "these things happened to them as an example, and they were written for our instruction, upon whom the ends of the ages have come" (1 Corinthians 10:11). Paul affirms that the journeys recorded in the Old Testament serve as *examples* to inform the lives of his hearers, and by extension, our lives as well (Romans 15:4; 1 Corinthians 10:6).

The Goal-Oriented Spiritual Journey Paradigm is the result of a systematic search of the examples God has given to us in the Scriptures. The Bible's narratives[1] of the lives of God's people contain not only moral and ethical lessons, but also lessons of how God actually relates to us as we journey through life. By examining the patterns that exist in the journeys of the Biblical characters, we gain insight into how God directs our own spiritual journeys.

Saving Egypt and His Family from Famine: Joseph's Journey

Joseph's goal-oriented spiritual journey as a leader in Egypt under the authority of Pharaoh finds its operative theme in Joseph's message to his brothers:

> "And now do not be grieved or angry with yourselves, because you sold me here; for God sent me before you to preserve life. For the famine has been in the land these two years, and there

27

are still five years in which there will be neither plowing nor harvesting. And God sent me before you to preserve for you a remnant in the earth, and to keep you alive by a great deliverance. Now, therefore, it was not you who sent me here, but God; and He has made me a father to Pharaoh and lord of all his household and ruler over all the land of Egypt." (Genesis 45:5-8)

In this reflection, Joseph acknowledges God's role in leading him to Egypt and in placing him on this tremendously significant journey. He looks beyond the superficial objective "facts" of his life to uncover the sovereign direction of the Lord in all that has befallen him.

The narrative asserts that Joseph was thirty years old when he received his call to deliver Egypt and his own family from famine (Genesis 41:46). His phase two experience involved interpreting Pharaoh's dream about the upcoming seven years of good harvest and seven years of famine (Genesis 41:1-32), delineating both the goal and methodology to meet the challenge of surviving the upcoming disaster (Genesis 41:33-36), and accepting the call from Pharaoh to perform this work (Genesis 41:37-45). No doubt Joseph accepted this mission because he discerned that God Himself was the sender of the dream and that it was He, and not just Pharaoh, who wanted him to assume the work (Genesis 41:32).

How did God prepare Joseph for such an awesome task (phase one)? Joseph's biographer begins the story of his journey to Egypt by relating that dreams played a significant role in influencing the course of Joseph's life. Phase one began thirteen years prior to Joseph's appearance before Pharaoh, when he was seventeen and angered his brothers by sharing his dreams with them (Genesis 37:2-11). This led his brothers to sell him into slavery, and eventually he ended up in Egypt (Genesis 37:18-36).

At this point, we must, as interpreters of the story, make a distinction between how Joseph experienced this episode and how the biographer intends for it to be understood. When Joseph related his dreams as a seventeen year old and subsequently found himself betrayed by his brothers, he did not say to himself, "I am doing this so that thirteen years from now I will be used by God to save Egypt and my family from famine." Such an understanding was beyond him at this point in his journey; this is why this phase is called an *unconscious* journey.

However, the chronicler of the journey apparently intends for us to see this episode as the beginning of Joseph's preparation for the task that would be revealed at a later time. Joseph is presented as a person who is carried along by events and forces that are not under his control. Not only is he sold into slavery against his will, but he is also thrown into prison unjustly (Genesis 39:19-23), where he is given an opportunity to interpret the chief cupbearer's and chief baker's dreams (Genesis 40:1-23) - a fortuitous event which ultimately leads him to a date with Pharaoh. In all of these experiences, the chronicler sees the hidden hand of the Lord, guiding Joseph to his destiny (Genesis 39:5, 21, 23). By God's grace and help, Joseph will discover the reason for his journey to Egypt. Joseph's phase one experience, therefore, is firmly under the control of God.

The course of Joseph's phase three experience is summarized in Genesis 41:46b-57. For the first seven years, he collected grain, and dispensed it throughout the seven years of famine. Thus, phase three lasted for 14 years and when the famine was past, his goal was reached (phase four). His phase five experience involves his reintegration into to the affairs of his family as a person who is very different from the teenager who was sold into slavery decades earlier.

Perhaps the most sublime lesson from Joseph's spiritual journey is that tragedies which seem to have no purpose can be mysteriously part of God's plan for a future goal-oriented journey. As the sovereign Lord of human history, God can transform calamities into pivotal journey milestones (Genesis 50:19-20; Romans 8:28).

Leading God's People to the Promised Land: Moses' Journey

Moses encountered his call from God (phase two) when he was eighty years old. God manifested His presence to Moses via a burning bush (Exodus 3:2-6) and then challenged Moses to embrace the task of liberating Israel from Pharaoh's oppressive rule:

And the LORD said, "I have surely seen the affliction of My people who are in Egypt, and have given heed to their cry because of their taskmasters, for I am aware of their sufferings. So I have come down to deliver them from the power of the Egyptians, and to bring them up from that land to a good and spacious land, to a land flowing with milk and honey, to the place of the Canaanite and the Hittite and the Amorite and the Perizzite and the Hivite and the Jebusite. And, now, behold, the cry of the sons of Israel has come to Me; furthermore, I have seen the oppression with which the Egyptians are oppressing them. Therefore, come now, and I will send you to Pharaoh, so that you may bring My people, the sons of Israel, out of Egypt." (Exodus 3:7-10)

The elements of the call are clear. The goal is to liberate Israel and bring them to their homeland. Moses receives both a journey destination and a call to minister to a target people. His new understanding of who God is, combined with a call that cannot be denied, propels Moses from his solitude as a shepherd into the center of a people's struggle for liberation and freedom.

Moses' response to the call is also worthy of note. Unlike Joseph, who seems to accept his call with ease and grace, Moses struggles with his qualifications to serve God in this capacity: "But Moses said to God, 'Who am I, that I should go to Pharaoh, and that I should bring the sons of Israel out of Egypt?'" (Exodus 3:11). In response, God affirms that He is in control and will lead Moses as he fulfills God's will (Exodus 3:12-4:9). Moses then reflects on and questions whether or not he has the spiritual gifts to fulfill God's mission, and God responds by promising that Moses will receive the necessary gifts and by *linking* Moses' journey to Aaron's:

Moses said to the LORD, "O Lord, I have never been eloquent, neither in the past nor since you have spoken to your servant. I am slow of speech and tongue." The LORD said to him, "Who gave man his mouth? Who makes him deaf or mute? Who gives him sight or makes him blind? Is it not I, the LORD? Now go; I will help you speak and will teach you what to say." But Moses said, "O Lord, please send someone else to do it." Then the LORD's anger burned against Moses and he said, "What about your brother, Aaron the Levite? I know he can speak well. He is

30

already on his way to meet you, and his heart will be glad when he sees you. You shall speak to him and put words in his mouth; I will help both of you speak and will teach you what to do. He will speak to the people for you, and it will be as if he were your mouth and as if you were God to him. But take this staff in your hand so you can perform miraculous signs with it." (Exodus 4:10-17)

In spite of Moses' humility, the outline of his life prior to the call demonstrates that God had prepared him for this ministry. Moses' phase one experience includes his fortuitous entry into Pharaoh's household as an infant (Exodus 2:1-10), the awakening of his sense of solidarity with his fellow Jews which led to his exile to Midian (Exodus 2:11-14), and the development of a close relationship with Jethro, who would later play an important role in Moses' phase three experience by providing sound advice (Exodus 2:16-22; 18:1-27).

The writer of Exodus also recognizes another dimension of phase one preparatory development. Beyond Moses' personal phase one experience lies a contextual journey that is *transpersonal*. Not only is Moses prepared to hear a call from God to reach a new goal, but the people and nations with whom he is to interact are also being prepared for his ministry. The transpersonal dimension of phase one is represented by the growth of oppression in Egypt (Exodus 1:8-22), the death of Pharaoh (Exodus 2:23), and the readiness of Israel to receive deliverance from God (Exodus 2:23-25).

Moses' phase three experience commences as Moses receives permission to leave Midian in order to travel to Egypt (Exodus 4:18). The rest of Exodus, and most of Numbers, Leviticus and Deuteronomy, record the winding course of his conscious ministry phase of the journey. Unlike Joseph's journey, phase three for Moses is filled with disappointments, delays and disasters caused by the sinful rebellion of the newly liberated community and his own unwise responses to their unfaithfulness.

The presence of sin was pervasive in Moses' conscious journey with the Israelites. Accordingly, the journey itself was stretched out to such a point that God was unwilling for Moses to experience the complete fulfillment of his journey goal (entering into the promised land). Nevertheless, a phase four experience is fully documented at the

31

end of Deuteronomy. Moses reflects on his journey and asserts that God has been active and present throughout its course (Deuteronomy 29:1-32:47). In a spirit of worship and recognition of God's majesty, power and grace, he blesses Israel (Deuteronomy 33:1-29), and then he actually experiences physical death (Deuteronomy 32:48-52; 34:1-7). Phase five for Moses involves entry into the afterlife (from a New Testament perspective).

Protecting God's People from Harm: Esther's Journey

The pivotal event in Esther's spiritual journey is the reception of God's call to protect the exiled Jewish nation. Her call arrives through the counsel of Mordecai:

> "Do not think that because you are in the king's house you alone of all the Jews will escape. For if you remain silent at this time, relief and deliverance for the Jews will arise from another place, but you and your father's family will perish. And who knows but that you have come to royal position for such a time as this?" (Esther 4:13-14)

In this phase two experience, Esther is confronted with a need (deliverance) and a target people whom she can assist (the Jews), and she must decide whether or not to accept responsibility for fulfilling the mission set before her. Mordecai, who acts as a *spiritual director* for Esther throughout the story (Esther 2:10, 20), obviously already senses that God has called Esther to this journey. In light of her initial coolness to the call (Esther 4:9-11), he warns her that there will be a penalty to pay for refusing the call ("you and your father's family will perish"). He also shares another important spiritual journey insight: when a person sins by refusing to accept a call, God will extend this call to another person ("if you remain silent at this time, relief and deliverance for the Jews will arise from another place"). The emergence of sin and disobedience even in a later phase of the spiritual journey can lead to the transference of the call; in Moses' case, he is replaced by Joshua before Israel enters the promised land.

How did God prepare Esther to receive this call to mission (phase one)? Before the call was revealed, Esther was given the gifts (or graces) of physical beauty (Esther 2:7), a willingness to listen and learn from others (Esther 2:10, 20), and an ability to favorably impress and get along with other people (Esther 2:9, 15, 17). By using these strengths, God was able to gain her entry into the royal household, a strategic place in which she would later be able to influence the king.

Esther 4:15-9:19 details how the queen cooperated with Mordecai and others to bring deliverance to the exiled people of God (phase three). The institution of a celebratory experience (the feast of Purim; Esther 9:20-10:32) indicates that Esther's journey goal has been reached successfully (phase four). Unfortunately (for our curiosity about Esther is left unsatisfied), the book does not indicate what Esther did after this specific goal-oriented journey was complete (phase five).

Taking Up the Cross of Salvation: Jesus' Journey

Jesus' three year ministry journey is an excellent example of the five phase goal-oriented spiritual journey process. His call to ministry at the time of His baptism (phase two) includes the revelation that He is God's Son, the Messiah of Israel:

> As soon as Jesus was baptized, he went up out of the water. At that moment heaven was opened, and he saw the Spirit of God descending like a dove and lighting on him. And a voice from heaven said, "This is my Son, whom I love; with him I am well pleased." (Matthew 3:16-17)

Although the goal of Jesus' ministry is not explicitly stated in Matthew's account, it would have been obvious to anyone familiar with Old Testament Messianic prophecy that the revelatory statement from heaven was related to Isaiah 42:1- "Behold, My Servant, whom I uphold; My chosen one in whom My soul delights. I have put My Spirit upon Him; He will bring forth justice to the nations" (see also Psalm 2:7-9). In John's account, John the Baptist proclaims the goal of Jesus' journey: "Behold, the Lamb of God who takes away the sin of the world!" (John 1:29).

By combining the testimonies of Isaiah and John, we understand that the goal of Jesus' ministry is to manifest God's justice (the

33

Kingdom of God) through the forgiveness of sins by sacrificing himself on the Cross. Jesus' target group consists of all the nations of the world, both Jews and Gentiles, although in practice the gospel went first to His own people (Romans 1:16-17).

The four Gospels are not birth to death biographical works in the modern Western sense, but rather recount Jesus' Messianic ministry journey. The Gospel accounts do not treat every detail of Jesus' life as equally significant. Instead, they emphasize phases three and four - Jesus' conscious journey towards His goal as the Messiah, and His reaching the goal by sacrificing Himself on the Cross.

Mark makes no attempt to record Jesus' life before His ministry call was received, and only takes three verses to describe the calling itself (Mark 1:9-11) before launching into the chronicle of Jesus' phase three ministry journey. John's brief reference to Jesus' phase one experience is a remarkable affirmation of Jesus' pre-existence and divinity (John 1:1-3).

Both John and Mark, however, join with Matthew and Luke in describing a significant contextual element of Jesus' phase one experience - John the Baptist's ministry (John 1:19- 28; Mark 1:2-8; Matthew 3:1-12; Luke 3:1-17). John's phase three ministry experience (his preaching of the gospel and baptizing) serves as an essential preparatory step for the launching of Jesus' own ministry by awakening Israel's yearnings for personal salvation, national redemption, and the revelation of their Messiah. John declares, "I am the voice of one crying in the wilderness, 'Make straight the way of the LORD,' as Isaiah the prophet said" (John 1:23).

Matthew records only those phase one events in Jesus' ministry journey which demonstrate that he was prepared by God to serve as Israel's Messiah. Writing to an audience with a Jewish background, he stresses Jesus' Davidic roots - an essential element in qualifying Jesus for the office of Messiah, the anointed king of God's chosen people (Matthew 1:1-17). He records Jesus' birth, where an angel affirms that Jesus has been sent to "save His people from their sins" (Matthew 1:21). Jesus' later phase two experience is not a product of His own egotistical desires, but a true call from God that had already been revealed to His parents. Likewise, the stories of the visit of the wise men, Herod's persecution, and the flight to and from Egypt (Matthew

34

2:1-23), all help to authenticate Jesus' ministry by demonstrating that God has sent Jesus in fulfillment of selected Old Testament prophecies.

Luke takes a different tack in describing Jesus' phase one experience. While also detailing the events that surround Jesus' birth (Luke 1:5-2:20), Luke alone relates a number of Jesus' personal experiences as a child. During his circumcision, Jesus' future ministry is affirmed by Simeon the prophet and Anna the prophetess (Luke 2:21-38). Once again, Jesus' call is acknowledged by other parties even before He personally receives it.

Yet Luke's truly unique contribution is still yet to come. He summarizes Jesus' preparatory experience twice in similar terms, and between them inserts one example - Jesus' visit to the Temple when he was twelve (Luke 2:41-51): "And the child grew and became strong; he was filled with wisdom; and the grace of God was upon Him. . . And Jesus grew in wisdom and stature, and in favor with God and men" (Luke 2:40, 52).

Luke maintains that Jesus' unconscious journey provides Him with the opportunity to mature by gaining strength, wisdom and the ability to relate to other people through God's grace - essential qualities for the Savior to have in order to fulfill His ministry. Luke's manner of categorizing Jesus' phase one experience as the progressive development of personal qualities is not unprecedented in Scripture. For example, God prepares Noah to accept the call to build the ark by guiding him into a lifestyle characterized by righteousness, integrity and an abiding sense of God's continuing presence (Genesis 6:9).

Matthew, Mark, and Luke all link the starting of Jesus' phase three experience (his conscious exercise of ministry) with the beginning of His public ministry (Matthew 4:17; Mark 1:14-15; Luke 4:14-21). John also does so, but his account (for stylistic reasons) seems to allow for two possible beginning points for phase three (John 1:36 and 2:11). The thrust of Jesus' phase three conscious journey phase is well-known. It may be simply summarized here as the proclamation and manifestation of the kingdom of God through preaching, healing, casting out of demons, and educating selected disciples as Jesus heads towards His goal of sacrificing Himself on the Cross.

Jesus' complex phase four experience includes the Last Supper (his good-bye to his disciples), Gethsemane (a prayerful expression of

His determination to remain faithful to the journey goal), His trial in both Jewish and Roman courts, and His actual death on Calvary (as a substitutionary atonement for humanity's sinfulness). Although these events all take place within a week of one another, they bring together all of the essential themes of Jesus' Messianic journey. The Cross is the consummation of everything he has been striving to achieve. Phase four, therefore, must never be seen as an inconsequential ending tacked on to the journey, but rather as its culmination and realization. Phase four is the heart of the journey, and not an afterthought.

Phase five (renewal and new life) begins on Easter Sunday, as the resurrected Jesus waits for for His next journey (His ascension to heaven) and new journey goals. In this phase, Jesus also brings the disciples' journeys to a proper conclusion (phase four). He meets with them, explains the true meaning of the journey he has just completed, and sets the stage for their next journey as an apostolic ministry group (Matthew 28:16-20; Luke 24:13-49; John 20:10-21:25). In Jesus' follow-up journey, He assumes His rightful place alongside the Father as Lord and Savior (Acts 3:21; 7:55-56; Philippians 2:9-11) and intercedes on behalf of the saints (Hebrews 1:3; 7:24-25; 9:24; 12:2). He is still living out this journey at the present time.

Extending the Gospel Beyond One's Own Community: Peter's Journey

The preceding journey examples (Joseph, Moses, Esther and Jesus), by the very grandeur, wide scope and length of time needed to complete the journey, may seem somewhat divorced from the kind of spiritual journeys most of us embrace.

We do not imagine that God is calling us to save an entire people, country, or for that matter, the human race, as we ponder how God wants us to serve Him. Therefore, the next two journey examples (Peter and Paul) concern short-term journeys which are more akin to the kinds of calls we experience today.

Acts 9:32-11:18 describes one of Peter's goal-oriented ministry journeys. Although it was short-term, it nevertheless had a profound impact on the development of the early church. In Acts 10:9-23, Peter

36

receives a phase two call from God to share the gospel with a person from another ethnic group:

> About noon the following day as they were on their journey and approaching the city, Peter went up on the roof to pray. He became hungry and wanted something to eat, and while the meal was being prepared, he fell into a trance. He saw heaven opened and something like a large sheet being let down to earth by its four corners. It contained all kinds of four-footed animals, as well as reptiles of the earth and birds of the air. Then a voice told him, "Get up, Peter. Kill and eat." "Surely not, Lord!" Peter replied. "I have never eaten anything impure or unclean." The voice spoke to him a second time, "Do not call anything impure that God has made clean." This happened three times, and immediately the sheet was taken back to heaven. (Acts 10:9-16)

God's call to Peter comes via a visionary trance which incorporates symbols that Peter either is unable to comprehend or unwilling to accept: "Peter was wondering about the meaning of the vision" (Acts 10:17a). We often experience both types of initial reaction when we enter into phase two of a new journey. However, Peter soon experiences the same call by a different means, and his journey goal and target group become clear to him. He is called to explain the Gospel to a single non-Jewish family in a nearby town:

> While Peter was still thinking about the vision, the Spirit said to him, "Simon, three men are looking for you. So get up and go downstairs. Do not hesitate to go with them, for I have sent them." Peter went down and said to the men, "I'm the one you're looking for. Why have you come?" The men replied, "We have come from Cornelius the centurion. He is a righteous and God-fearing man, who is respected by all the Jewish people. A holy angel told him to have you come to his house so that he could hear what you have to say." (Acts 10:19-22)

Peter's call did not emerge in a vacuum. God sovereignly leads both Cornelius and Peter in ways that prepare Peter to accept the above call to reach across a significant ethnic boundary. Peter's phase one experience involves God leading Cornelius to be open to hearing about a Savior who is not of his own race, and instructing him through a vision to invite Peter to his house for the purpose of hearing God's good news (Acts 10:1-8). In Peter's own personal journey, God leads him to preach in Joppa (Acts 9:32-43) so that he will be accessible to Cornelius' emissaries. Furthermore, Peter's ministry journey up to this point places him in a unique position to bring the Gospel to the Gentile community. As the leader of the church in its infancy, he can authenticate this revolutionary development, even as he did when the Samaritans received the Gospel during one of his previous journeys (Acts 8:14-24).

Peter begins the conscious phase (phase three) of this particular journey when he befriends Cornelius' messengers and travels with them to speak to Cornelius in Caesarea (Acts 10:23-24). He shares the good news of Christ's life, death and resurrection with Cornelius and his family, who receive the message with faith and experience the power and presence of the Holy Spirit. The ministry goal is reached when Peter baptizes Cornelius's family (Acts 10:34-48).

Peter's phase four experience continues as he reports to the other "apostles and the brethren who were throughout Judea" (Acts 11:1) in Jerusalem. His reflective sharing about how God had guided him in this specific goal-oriented journey leads the whole leadership into a new understanding of what God is doing in the world around them. They cease criticizing Peter and instead praise God (Acts 11:2-18). With his goal completed, Peter then moves on to other ministry level goal-oriented journeys (phase five).

The Macedonian Call for Help: Paul's Journey

Sometimes, the call to a goal-oriented journey involves traveling to a new geographical location. Jonah is sent to Nineveh. Philip travels to Samaria. A present day pastor crosses a state line as he or she concludes one pastoral journey and begins another. A team of lay people leave their home town to serve on a short-term missions project in another country.

This is true not only of journeys that are years in length, but also of short-term experiences. For every Abraham that is called to leave home permanently to journey to his promised land, there is a Paul who is called to go temporarily to a new location in order to accomplish God's will.

One of Paul's short-term goal-oriented spiritual journeys now is known as the Second Missionary Journey. His famous phase two experience is called the Macedonian vision:

> During the night Paul had a vision of a man of Macedonia standing and begging him, "Come over to Macedonia and help us." After Paul had seen the vision, we got ready at once to leave for Macedonia, concluding that God had called us to preach the gospel to them. (Acts 16:9-10)

There is nothing unusual in this phase two experience. Through a vision, Paul and his band discover a goal and a target group. They are called to preach the gospel in Europe, beginning with the Macedonians.

Paul's phase one experience, however, does break some new ground for our analysis. First, before receiving the Macedonian call, Paul parts company with Barnabas and Mark and teams up with Silas and Timothy (Acts 15:37-16:1). *Developing new relationships and partnerships is a common phase one experience.* As new people enter into our lives and as others part company with us, new possibilities for future ministry may be fashioned by God, even though we cannot guess how these new relationships will affect our future. Second, Luke records a seemingly bizarre action of the Holy Spirit:

> Paul and his companions traveled throughout the region of Phrygia and Galatia, having been kept by the Holy Spirit from preaching the word in the province of Asia. When they came to the border of Mysia, they tried to enter Bithynia, but the Spirit of Jesus would not allow them to. So they passed by Mysia and went down to Troas. (Acts 16:6-8)

As the unconscious phase of a journey comes to a close, God often causes us to question what we are doing by denying us permission to continue the journey. This seemingly negative process encourages us to search for a new call, clarifies existing options, and narrows the field of choices. In Paul's journey, this leads him to camp in Troas, a shore town opposite Macedonia, where his new call is issued.

We could argue that this action of the Holy Spirit belongs to phase two of the spiritual journey paradigm. I prefer to see it as a concluding feature of phase one, since this activity serves to prepare us to receive a call but does not contain the call in and of itself.

Furthermore, we tend to feel frustrated, anxious, confused and directionless, and these are the very feelings that often signal the beginning of the conclusion of phase one. The feelings associated with phase two (such as excitement, self-doubt, surprise, awe of God, etc.) are usually quite different.

Phase three of Paul's second missionary journey (Acts 16:11-18:21) contains numerous highlights. The first convert in Europe, Lydia, accepts Christ (Acts 16:14-15) and the Philippian jailor and his family also convert (Acts 16:27-34). Paul ministers in Thessalonica, Berea, Athens, Corinth and Ephesus (Acts 17:1-18:20).

Having reached his goal of establishing a foothold for the Gospel in Europe (phase four), Paul returns to Antioch (Acts 18:22), where this journey began (Acts 15:30-36). Phase five (renewal and new life) serves to separate the second from the third missionary journeys and is acknowledged by Luke when he says that Paul "spent some time" in Antioch (Acts 18:23).

The Two Levels of Goal-Oriented Spiritual Journeys

There are two levels of goal-oriented spiritual journeys which need to be distinguished so that we may understand their relationship to one another. The distinction lies in the differing goals which spiritual journeys may have.

Redemptive-level spiritual journeys embrace *goals related to personal or corporate wholeness and spiritual growth.* Such journeys enable us to express the redemptive application of Christ's work in our lives. We travel toward an existential realization of Christ's healing and wisdom in order to become more psychologically whole and spiritually mature.

The redemptive-level spiritual journey progresses according to the five phases we have already described. The story of Job serves as the ideal model for this level of spiritual journeying. Job's phase one and two experiences are briefly described in the prologue (Job 1-2). Most of the drama concerns phase three, as Job suffers through his "dark night of the soul" and subsequently receives the wisdom of God (Job

40

3-41). Phase four is succinctly covered in the recording of Job's final speech to God (Job 42:1-6). The epilogue is a summary of Job's phase five experiences (Job 42:7-16).

Job's redemptive-level spiritual journey illustrates the principle that our growth sometimes necessitates the experiencing of a temporary, and painful, alienation from God (Job 7:11-21; 23:15-17) and others (for example, Job's three friends) so that our perspective may be broadened and deepened (Job 38-42). This level of journeying often involves a crisis of faith in response to the insecurities manifested by having to adjust to changing relational patterns. The apparent experience of alienation from God and others is not caused by one's personal sin (although sin may cause other manifestations of alienation), as Job plaintively protests. Rather, it is a test designed to expose hidden motives and "lighten" the soul from its earthly attachments so that it may continue its pilgrimage toward God.

Accordingly, one of the basic principles of the redemptive-level spiritual journey is that *the suffering of the innocent is surgery for the soul.* Job reminds us that the suffering of the righteous is not an accident, nor a judgment, but part of the mysterious will of God. Therefore, when we are called to such a journey, we should embrace such experiences as authentic and redemptive spiritual journey encounters with God (Job 2:10). As Christ says, "The Son of Man must suffer many things. . . If anyone would come after me, he must deny himself and take up his cross daily and follow me" (Luke 9:22-23). As we embrace our times of suffering which have come to us through no fault of our own, we identify with the mystery of Christ's life and death, who suffered through His own dark night from Gethsemane to the Cross to bring us God's redemptive power and new life.

How, then, should the righteous suffer when they are called to embrace a redemptive-level journey? Based in part on his understanding of Job's journey, James exhorts his readers to face their suffering by exercising perseverance and patience in light of the hope of receiving God's compassion and mercy (James 5:7-12). Faith expresses itself through these two virtues, and the gaining of wisdom is the reward of the journey (James 1:2-12). Thus, exercising patience and perseverance is essential to the progress of our spiritual journeys:

"Perseverance must finish its work so that you may be mature and complete, not lacking anything" (James 1:4).

The Biblical examples of goal-oriented journeys in this chapter (excluding Job's) are *mission-level* spiritual journeys. The goal or task of the mission-level spiritual journey is not centered on oneself, but on *ministering to other people for the sake of the Kingdom of God*. The mission-level spiritual journey is not primarily concerned with one's own personal growth in holiness or psychological maturity, but instead with facilitating growth in others through service.

The redemptive-level spiritual journey is not an end unto itself, but rather a prelude for the mission level of spiritual journeying. Experiencing spiritual journeys solely on the redemptive level is not sufficient for a full Christian life. Christ redeems men and women not just for their own sake, but also for an other-centered reason, which is to expand the Kingdom of God by accepting journeys of ministry and service to others in His name.

The redemptive and mission levels, linked together, express God's sovereignty, love, grace and vision for our lives, and are to be celebrated and appreciated as wonderful gifts. The redemptive level is *foundational* to the mission level and its journeys function as necessary preliminary experiences (phase one) for those who encounter a call to mission-oriented journeys. We make a serious mistake when we are satisfied with only experiencing redemptive-level journeys, and an equally serious mistake when we neglect this foundational level by stressing only service to others.

Straddling the Levels: Friendships and Other Relational Journeys

Thus far, relationships have been seen as playing a role in both redemptive and mission level spiritual journeys. Relationships impact journeys in several ways. The coming and going of relationships often coincide with the beginning and ending of journeys. Links between people are essential if phase three of our journeys are to be successful. Destructive relationships can lead to significant delays in reaching journey goals.

It is also possible to see relationships as spiritual journeys in their own right, apart from how they assist redemptive or mission-level journeys. As our relationships grow and deepen, and then often ebb, we can discern the same five phase progression taking place. God prepares us for relationships even before we commit to pursuing them (phase one). The relationships we experience are covenantal in nature, requiring commitment as we pursue the goals of closeness, fidelity, self-revelation, mutual acceptance, trust, and love (phase two). Relationships require cooperation to flourish (phase three). Relationships come to an end (phase four), due to biological (death), preferential (deciding one does not wish to continue the relationship), or circumstantial (moving away) reasons. Ideally, the ending of relationships involves the phase four characteristics of grieving and reflection. Old relationships pave the way for new ones (phase five).

At first glance, these observations would seem to indicate that relational spiritual journeys should be accorded the status of a level, like redemptive and mission-level journeys. However, relational journeys perhaps are better seen as straddling the boundary between the redemptive and mission levels for two reasons.

First, relational journeys are neither primarily self-centered like redemptive journeys, nor primarily other-centered like mission journeys, but are clearly both at the same time. Relationships require a continual balancing act between the other and the self. This balancing act is of central importance to the course of the journey, and often helps to define its nature and potential. Thus, relational journeys are simultaneously redemptive and mission-oriented, just as light is both a particle and a wave at the same time.

Second, it is often difficult to define what a relationship's ultimate goal is at the conscious start of a relational journey . Thus, when two people (male and female) meet and decide to become friends (phase two), they usually cannot discern immediately whether God has called them to be casual acquaintances, close friends, or marriage partners. Only time, and the progression of the relationship, will make God's will clear.

Although we can and should analyze our relationships as goal-oriented journeys, on a theoretical level, such journeys are best understood as occupying a spiritual zone between the two levels we

43

have outlined. Like elusive subatomic particles which exist but cannot be precisely positioned because of their motion, relational journeys may mysteriously move from one level to the other, or exist in both at the same time, in a rather indeterminate manner. And honestly, I would have it no other way, for this preserves the wondrous mystery of the relational adventure!

Chapter Three

God Calls Churches to Journey, Too!

The Church is Like a Caravan

Vernard Eller visualizes the church as a *caravan*, which he defines as "a group of people banded together to make *common cause* in seeking a *common destination*."[1] In contrast to the "commissary model" of the church, in which the institution's purpose is to "dispense particular goods, services, or benefits to a select constituency," the caravaning church model emphasizes community over institution, and encourages journeying over waiting for "customers" to come to the storehouse of spiritual goods."[2] It is a dynamic image of the people of God journeying in response to God's call.

Caravaning, or journeying, is not an end in itself. The church is on the move not for the sake of movement, but in order to manifest lifestyle patterns which "confirm its *commitment to the mission of God* and the establishment of his Kingdom."[3] In chronicling the difficult transition to a mission-oriented journey model of church life and witness among the members of the Church of the Savior in Washington, D.C., Elizabeth O'Connor affirms that its pastor "walked with the sureness of one headed for a far better place" even though some members had fears or concerns:

Gordon Cosby still feels that the churches, in their quest for structures that nurture life in people, must know that they are venturing into new territory, and that the resources for their exploration rest in the tremendous untapped potential of their own people. The difficulty is that we so often lack confidence in ourselves and in our companions and search for the answers in some other place.[4]

The Goal-Oriented Spiritual Journey Paradigm can provide us with that missing confidence because it charts congregational journeying. Congregations that want to respond to God's call but don't know how to reach the destination God has ordained for them can employ its five phase model as a basis for discovering and affirming God's will.

A congregation's spiritual journey can be analyzed from two perspectives. The *person-centered perspective* considers each individual's spiritual journey as its central concern and essentially values the group as a spiritual support system. In contrast, the *communal perspective* affirms that a local church's spiritual journey is not merely the aggregate of all of its individual members' journeys. A church is called as a singular entity (a body) to journey toward goals that are not identical to any one individual's or subgroup's goals. In this perspective, individuals commit themselves to helping the church community fulfill its goals in obedience to God's call. We allow our individual journeys to be linked to the larger, more inclusive, collective journey of the group as a whole.

Although they stand in dynamic tension with one another, both perspectives must be affirmed and recognized as vital to the healthy functioning of a congregation. In this chapter, we will provide Scriptural examples of both perspectives and analyze them in light of the Goal-Oriented Spiritual Journey Paradigm.

Joining Together to Fulfill Our Personal Journeys

God calls people to join together in order to fulfill their personal spiritual journeys. The contemporary church affirms this by supporting the formation of various kinds of small, relationally-oriented support, self-help and Bible study groups. Growth groups, Alcoholics Anonymous, Weight Watchers and the Wednesday night Bible study all share in common the underlying principle that the group serves its individual members by providing them with the support, knowledge and resources that they need to fulfill their personal journey goals. The group exists for the benefit of its individuals.

When we join together to fulfill a personal need or call, the journey of the resulting group can be understood in the same way that individual journeys can. The Bible does not provide us with many descriptions of small group journeys, but one stands out as an archetypal model - the small group of disciples that Jesus formed during his earthly ministry.

The discovery process (phase two) for a group's spiritual journey involves two aspects - *inclusion and call*. *Inclusion* denotes the recruitment of group members. This aspect of phase two of the apostolic band's life begins with the inviting of Peter, Andrew, James and John (Matthew 4:18-22; Mark 1:16-20; Luke 5:1-11), continues with Matthew's inclusion (Matthew 9:9-17; Mark 2:14-22; Luke 5:27-38) and presumably others whose stories are not told, and concludes with the formal formation of the discipleship group (Matthew 10:1-4; Mark 3:13-19; Luke 6:12-16).

Inclusion into the life of a group assumes either the prior acceptance of a call (which then motivates a person to join) or an acceptance of a call at the time of inclusion. Mark records both the inclusion and call of the disciples: "And He went up to the mountain and summoned those whom He Himself wanted, and they came to Him. And He appointed twelve, that they might be with Him, and that He might send them out to preach, and to have authority to cast out the demons" (Mark 3:13-15).

There are three reasons for the group's formation (its call), according to Mark's shorthand account. First, Jesus wants the disciples to journey with Him in order to receive spiritual instruction (cf. Matthew 10:5). For the disciples, this is a redemptive journey. Second, they are to be a support group for one another as they practice proclaiming the kingdom of God. Third, they are to support one another as they gain experience in dealing with the spiritual realm (healing the sick and demon-possessed).

We previously noted that a call contains not only a task, but also a target group that will benefit from the ministry. Matthew's account supplies both:

> These twelve Jesus sent out after instructing them, saying, "Do not go in the way of the Gentiles, and do not enter any city of the Samaritans; but rather go to the lost sheep of the house of Israel. And as you go, preach, saying, 'The kingdom of heaven is at hand.' Heal the sick, raise the dead, cleanse the lepers, cast out demons; freely you received, freely give." (Matthew 10:5-8)

47

We know little about how God prepared the twelve original disciples for their group journey experience (phase one), but there is one incident which provides evidence that Jesus discerned a connection between the disciples' past experience and present call: "And as He was going along by the Sea of Galilee, He saw Simon and Andrew, the brother of Simon, casting a net into the sea; for they were fishermen. And Jesus said to them, "Follow Me, and I will make you become fishers of men." And they immediately left their nets and followed Him" (Mark 1:16-18).

The only other personal call to journey with Jesus' group that is recorded in the Synoptics involves Matthew (Matthew 9:9; Mark 2:14; Luke 5:27-28). Besides his lineage (he was the son of Alpheus), all we know of Matthew is his prior occupation - he was a tax-collector. This occupation provided Matthew with skills that made him well-suited him to serve possibly as the recorder of the group's journey. Thus, in both cases, the prior occupations of the disciples prepared them for the ministry journey that lay ahead.

The conscious phase (phase three) of the group's journey involves an alternating pattern of teaching and practice. For example, in Mark 6, Jesus instructs the disciples (6:8-9), provides them with a ministry assignment (6:10-11), and sends them out to minister (6:12-13). When their ministry is completed, they return to the group to share their experiences and to rest (6:30-31).

Each teaching/practice cycle within the overall phase three period is experienced as a short-term goal-oriented journey by each individual disciple. I label this *journey within a journey* experience during phase three a *micro-level journey*. We often experience phase three as a sequence of individual spiritual journeys, each of which builds upon the results of the earlier individual journeys. Just as each year has four seasons, or fifty-two weeks, phase three can be broken down into constituent parts.

Phase three of the apostolic group's spiritual journey lasts for approximately three years and ends symbolically with the serving of the Last Supper (Matthew 26:26-35; Mark 14:22-25; Luke 22:17-20). Jesus, having taught the disciples all they need to know to minister in His absence, begins the process of disengaging Himself from the group and preparing for his own upcoming personal struggle. In a spiritually healthy group, phase four experience is often initiated by the leader, who takes his/her cue to announce that the group's journey is coming to a close from an inner acknowledgement that God is calling him/her to leave the group. It is also possible for phase four to be initiated by the other members of the group.

Phase four is experienced by the group members as a death experience. In the case of the apostolic group, the leader's death is physical, but usually the death experience involves simply the reaching of a group's journey goals. When this occurs, the reason for the group's existence is called into question. This can lead to the dissolution of the group or to a reorganization of the group around a new journey goal. The latter possibility describes the dynamics surrounding the apostolic small group. Jesus' death and departure symbolizes the ending of the apostles' journey as learners and they reorganize around the new call to be the evangelical leaders of the emerging post-resurrection church (Matthew 28:16-20; Acts 1:6-8).

After Jesus' arrest and death, His disciples went into hiding, and this relatively passive journey style is a primary indicator that phase five has begun. Having completed a journey, it is not necessary to enter into new activity immediately. Phase five often involves waiting for new direction while gathering strength for the next journey. We ordinarily need time to discern a new call. Time is also needed for the environment around us (people, historical movements, etc.) to enter into a proper alignment so that a new call may be received from God.

Phase five for the apostolic group begins when the encounter the resurrected Jesus. His post-resurrection appearances teach them truths that are foundational to their new call. This phase five experience is also a phase one (preparatory) time for them in relation to their new call, as Luke implies:

> To these He also presented Himself alive, after His suffering, by many convincing proofs, appearing to them over a period of forty days, and speaking of the things concerning the kingdom of God. And gathering them together, He commanded them not to leave Jerusalem, but to *wait* for what the Father had promised. (Acts 1:3-4).

The Sum Really is More Than Its Parts

It was not long before the followers of Jesus grew from a few dozen initial disciples to multiplied thousands throughout the Roman empire. Congregations founded by the apostles and other evangelists were different than the original apostolic small group. Rather than being a closed, temporary group, the local congregation represents a dynamic permanent model of the new society of human beings who have experienced the reconciling power of Jesus Christ in a specific locality. People called into the new society commit themselves to the selfless serving of others by placing their spiritual gifts and other resources at the disposal of the community (Acts 2:42-47; 4:32-37). To claim Jesus as Lord means to give oneself totally to His community so that, in cooperation with others, God's will might be fulfilled through the journey of the church.

The local church, as a body of believers, possesses an identity that transcends the individuals who comprise the fellowship. Congregations take on a collective persona based on their cultural setting, normative traditions and past history that cannot be identified with any individual person within the fellowship. For example, the seven churches in Revelation 2-3 are addressed as if each one were an individual entity responsible for its particular journey. Some of the churches were not faithful in the journeys, while others were more faithful in responding to God's call. Such a judgment did not mean that every individual within an unfaithful church was rejecting God's call in their own personal journeys (for example, Revelation 2:24 states there were a faithful few to be found in the Thyatiran church); rather, the church as a corporate entity was failing in its journey.

In both the Old and New Testaments, God calls His people as a collective entity to journey toward specific and definable goals. These goals are not identical to individual journey goals but are geared specifically to the group's life. The call to inhabit the promised land during the Exodus journey is directed to the community as a whole, and can only be fulfilled by the entire community as a singular entity. In the book of Judges, Israel is pictured as going through a series of trans-generational journeys, evidencing a progressively downward spiraling pattern of unfaithfulness to God, punishment and recommitment. In both Ezekiel and Hosea, the Jewish people are symbolically referred to as a woman who has betrayed her faithful husband.

In the New Testament, we catch snapshots of congregational corporate journeys. The epistles which are addressed to congregations provide us with pastoral responses to issues within the local church. Most of these issues (use of spiritual gifts, unity, expressing consideration and love for others, holiness) may be understood as manifestations of the typical phase three problem - lack of cooperation between people whose spiritual journeys have been linked by God. Analytical appraisals of the church's spiritual journeys tend to be limited to reminders of the church's call to be God's people and evangelical agents for the sake of the kingdom of God.

Historical accounts are the best means of preserving the flow of a community's spiritual journeys. In the New Testament, we possess only one historical survey of the early church, the book of Acts. Unfortunately, Acts does not focus on the journeys of specific local congregations, since it largely follows the ministries of the early church's two most influential leaders, Peter and Paul. There are a few exceptions, however. During the formative period of the Jerusalem church, the apostolic leadership sensed that God wanted to empower certain members of the congregation in order to meet the needs of one of the segments of the church:

> Now at this time while the disciples were increasing in number, a complaint arose on the part of the Hellenistic Jews against the native Hebrews, because their widows were being overlooked in the daily serving of food. And the twelve summoned the congregation of the disciples and said, "It is not desirable for us to neglect the word of God in order to serve tables. But select from among you, brethren, seven men of good reputation, full of the Spirit and of wisdom, whom we may put in charge of this task. But we will devote ourselves to prayer, and to the ministry of the word." And the statement found approval with the whole congregation; and they chose Stephen, a man full of faith and of the Holy Spirit, and Philip, Prochorus, Nicanor, Timon, Parmenas and Nicolas, a proselyte from Antioch. And these they brought before the apostles; and after praying, they laid their hands on them. (Acts 6:1-6)

51

In this episode, God's call contains both a task-specific goal (the charitable serving of food) and a target group (widows who were in need of assistance). The call is mediated through the apostles who place responsibility on the laity to find among themselves seven people who have the requisite gifts and personal qualities to accept this ministry challenge (Acts 6:3).

Several *communal perspective* journey principles may be discerned from this story. First, the apostles, though hearing the call and obviously accepting it as God's will for the church, did not take it upon themselves to actually fulfill this journey. Instead, they exhorted the body of Christ in their locality to discover people who were called to this particular ministry. The apostles, as responsible leaders, did not usurp the role that their people should play in building up the church's ministry. All too often in the contemporary church, it is assumed that new ministries will be staffed by leadership (board members and pastoral staff). This is a negation of the doctrine of the priesthood of all believers. From the communal perspective of a church's journey, it is imperative that leadership serve as mediators, authenticators, validators and supporters of prospective journeys, and not always as performers of the journey tasks.

Second, the apostolic advice to the congregation took into account that people are not called to new ministries without preparation (phase one). The prospective candidates had to have a good reputation and had already demonstrated that they were "full of the Spirit and of wisdom" (Acts 6:3).

Third, it should be noted that the process of calling forth people to accept this journey did not involve asking for volunteers, but rather involved a selection process based on spiritual discernment. The question was not "Who would like to do this job?" but rather "Who has God selected from among us to do this job?".

Fourth, the seven people who received and accepted God's call to serve food were prayed over and set aside for this ministry task (a communal embracing of the results of phase two). The Jerusalem church considered this ministry to be as spiritual as the ministry of teaching and preaching.

The congregation in Antioch, a model church, receives a good deal of attention in Acts. It records two instances in which the Antiochan church recognized a call from God to fulfill a ministry task. The first concerns the collection of a love offering:

> Now at this time some prophets came down from Jerusalem to Antioch. And one of them named Agabus stood up and began to indicate by the Spirit that there would certainly be a great famine all over the world. And this took place in the reign of Claudius. And in the proportion that any of the disciples had means, each of them determined to send a contribution for the relief of the brethren living in Judea. And this they did, sending it in charge of Barnabas and Saul to the elders. (Acts 11:27-30)

In this instance, the prophet Agabus serves as a *ministry initiator*, the person who alerts a congregation to a call from God. The call has both a task and a target group: the Antiochans are asked to raise fund for famine relief for the benefit of the Judean faithful. Although Acts does not explicitly make the connection, we may surmise that the church was prepared by God (phase one) to receive Agabus' call in a positive manner through the teaching ministry of Barnabas and Saul (Acts 11:22-26). These two men both had ties to the Judean church and certainly would have helped the Antiochan Gentiles (Acts 11:20-21) to appreciate their spiritual kinship with the Judean Christians. Having discovered the need and accepting it (phase two), the Antiochan Christians raised money and sent Barnabas and Saul to deliver it to the needy churches (phase three). The ministry journey comes to a close when the offering is dispensed and Antioch's representatives return home (phase four).

The second instance concerns the setting apart of Saul and Barnabas for their first missionary journey:

> Now there were at Antioch, in the church that was there, prophets and teachers: Barnabas, and Simeon who was called Niger, and Lucius of Cyrene, and Manaen who had been brought up with Herod the tetrarch, and Saul. And while they were ministering to the Lord and fasting, the Holy spirit said, "Set apart for Me Barnabas and Saul for the work to which I have called them." Then, when they had fasted and prayed and laid their hands on them, they sent them away. (Acts 13:1-3)

Prophets again play a key role in initiating a ministry journey in the local church. Their assent affirms that the call is authentically

53

from the Lord, and that it is the result of God's initiative (as opposed to Barnabas' or Saul's desires). Certainly, we also may affirm that the encouraging of churches to discover and accept God's call to journey is part of the prophetic ministry in the contemporary church as well, and that this prophetic function should be found among the leaders who have been called by God to guide their flock.

The Antiochan leaders discovered (phase two) God's desire to have them send forth Barnabas and Saul as missionaries to Jews in other unreached Jewish settlements (Acts 13:4-14:25). The leaders had been prepared (phase one) to accept such a responsibility by the duo's prior teaching ministry among them and by the successful journey Barnabas and Saul had undertaken during the famine (Acts 11:22-30).

As Barnabas and Saul worked together to fulfill God's call (phase three), an unanticipated change of direction took place in their ministry journey. Due to the opposition of their Jewish hearers (Acts 13:44-52), they decided to reach out to the Gentiles instead (a change in target groups). This is not an uncommon occurrence in phase three of spiritual journeys. God often provides us with an *initial goal* that serves to inspire us to begin journeying. This enticement to journey places us in a context or position to receive the *ultimate goal*, which is a fuller expression of God's purpose. Often, but not always, this goal transition during phase three is accompanied by a *covenant renewal* experience.

As the missionaries reflected on the significance of their ministry journey (phase four), the opening of a witness to the Gentiles came to be seen as their primary achievement: "And when they had arrived and gathered the church together, they began to report all things that God had done with them and how He had opened a door of faith to the Gentiles" (Acts 14:27).

Congregational Spiritual Journeys

The dynamics of group journeys are much more complex than those experienced on an individual level. This is because a group's spiritual journey is a collective expression of a number of individual journeys that have been linked together by God in ways that may or may not be readily apparent as the congregation's journey proceeds.

Therefore, the description of a group's journey must take into account the relationship between the group and each individual.

There are two ways to describe the course of a group's spiritual journey and its relationship to individual journeys. The first follows the reception of God's call as it is mediated throughout the various organizational levels of a congregation. The second emphasizes the interplay between the spiritual journeys of individuals within the group and how the linking of these journeys is reflected in and through the spiritual journey of the group as a whole.

A Church's Response to the Call of God

When a church receives a call from God to embrace a fresh spiritual journey and thus to accept a new ministry goal, its response may be seen to involve three related levels of activity: *a ministry initiator receives a call from God, the church leadership affirms the call, and the congregation embraces that call.*

The first level involves the personal journey of a *ministry or journey initiator.* This person may be the pastor, a board member or any other individual within the congregation. The ministry initiator is the person through whom God initially reveals the new ministry goal.

The reception of this call from God involves the ministry initiator in a spiritual journey that progresses according to the five phases of the Goal-Oriented Spiritual Journey Paradigm. He/she is prepared by the Lord through various life experiences (phase one) to be able to hear God's call and to understand it. Having received the call, and sensing its implications for church life, the ministry initiator accepts the responsibility of expressing this vision to the church (phase two). Phase three involves taking this vision to people who have the discernment to evaluate its validity and the authority to begin the implementation process. Usually this involves taking the vision to the leadership of the church.

The ministry initiator's spiritual journey goal is reached when leadership or another subgroup within the church validates the call and acts upon it (phase four). Having completed his or her journey, the ministry initiator embarks upon phase five (new life) which may

55

involve either ending any connection with this particular vision ("I'm moving on to something new") or getting further involved in the actual implementation of the journey.

The second level involves the leadership of the church. Phase one of the leadership's journey encompasses phases one and two of the ministry initiator's journey. The latter's preparation and reception of a new ministry vision sets the stage for God to be able to reveal to the leadership His will for the church. The leaders who respond to the ministry initiator's journey must be personally prepared through appropriate life experiences if they are to catch the vision.

The leadership enters into phase two (discovery) as the ministry initiator shares the vision with them. The initiator's phase three experience coincides with the leadership's phase two; he/she cooperates with God by leading his or her hearers into a discovery of a new call process. If the leadership accepts the vision as valid, they in turn will seek to help the congregation as a whole discover the vision (phase three). When the congregation affirms the call of God by accepting the challenge to journey, the leadership has reached its goal of incorporating the call of God into the spiritual journey of the church (phase four). As the congregation "takes the ball and runs with it", the leadership is then set free to move on to other areas (phase five).

The third level of activity involves the congregation's corporate journey. They are prepared for receiving the new call to ministry in the same way as the leadership. They accumulate a reservoir of life experiences that predisposes them to respond favorably to the call. The congregation's phase one experience embraces the ministry initiator's phases one, two and three and the leadership's phases one and two. God prepares the congregation to receive a new call to ministry by first having its leadership affirm the vision.

When the leadership brings the call to the attention of the congregation, the people of the church must respond to the vision on two levels (phase two). First, they must affirm that the proposed ministry or project is God's will for them at this time. Second, individuals within the congregation must hear and accept a call from God to perform the ministry. It is incongruous for a congregation to affirm a call in principle while lacking people who testify that God has called them to take responsibility for the ministry. If no one senses a call to ministry, then phase two has not been completed, or the proposed journey is not really God's will.

The congregation makes a transition from phase two to phase three as they affirm and empower those who have personally appropriated the call to fulfill their mission. The outworking of the ministry idea and the actual performance of ministry tasks are the essence of phase three activity. People involved in the ministry cooperate with the Holy Spirit, with other ministry team people and with the congregation at large, through the use of their spiritual gifts. When such activity takes place, leadership enters into phase four, having reached their journey goal of helping the congregation to embrace and fulfill God's will in this particular area.

Phase four of the congregational journey begins when the goals of the ministry have been reached. Once the congregation has reflected upon their ministry experiences and thanked God for them, then they will be ready to enter into new experiences of ministry (phase five), as God continues to lead them.

A properly implemented journey depends on *the ministry initiator being one phase ahead of the leadership, whose journey in turn must also be one phase ahead of the congregation's journey.* If a congregation launches into ministry without allowing the process to work itself out, errors that could have been avoided will be made (in terms of timing, defining objectives, etc.). The vision could become so distorted that it bears little resemblance to God's will. Further, the unity of the congregation could be threatened in a journey process that does not allow the vision to be communicated through the three levels outlined above.

Perhaps the most common error churches experience in working through the implications of a potential call to ministry from God is to ignore the part that the congregation at large is to play in accepting a call. This usually manifests itself when leadership boards or pastoral staff not only initiate and validate new ministries, but also assume that they have been called by God to perform the actual ministry work. This prevents people in the church from exercising their gifts as ministers of the Lord. This is not only a denial of the doctrine of the priesthood of all believers, but it is also a major reason why leaders burn out so often in our congregations. All people are called by God to embrace journeys in fulfillment of their responsibility as children of God and as members of a local church. Leadership (both pastoral and lay) are called by God to assist their flock in discovering and embracing their journeys, and not to usurp their place by performing the ministry that was meant for others (Ephesians 4:11-13).

The Dynamic Linking of
Our Spiritual Journeys

Two Pauline metaphors speak powerfully of the dynamic linking of the spiritual journeys of the people of God. Paul refers to the church as the body of Christ, composed of many different but equal members (1 Corinthians 12). The different parts of the body are at the same time independent and dependant on each other. Although the hand and the eye have different functions (which will cause them to embrace differing spiritual journeys), their actions affect each other.

In Ephesians 2, the church is likened to a building composed of many individual bricks which, when placed together, create the house of God. In like manner, as our individual spiritual journeys are linked through the foresight and wisdom of God, the collective spiritual journeys of the Christian community begin to manifest themselves.

These two metaphors preserve both the individual integrity and the communal inter-relatedness of the church and its individual members. The same holds true when we speak of the spiritual journeys that we experience. Each person embarks on a personal spiritual journey which is at the same time linked to the individual journeys of other Christians and to the church as a whole. My sense of being called to a journey impacts both the spiritual journeys of other people and the collective spiritual journey of the church to which I belong.

The corporate spiritual journey of the church *anchors* each person's individual journey and also *mediates* between the journeys of its members. The church's journey provides each individual with a sociological context (i.e., history and tradition) and a doctrinal/theological environment which serve to anchor the individual's journey within the Christian framework. No individual journey is acted out in isolation. Every spiritual journey is linked to others' journeys in ways that are sometimes explicit but more often hidden from us until the church as mediator draws out the hidden spiritual connections.

As the spiritual leader of the congregation, a pastor/spiritual director often articulates on behalf of the community of faith how individual journeys are linked, and thus fulfills the church's mediatorial role. Other members of the congregation may do so as well, if they possess the proper gifts of discernment.

In order to describe the dynamic process of how an individual's call to ministry impacts the spiritual journey of the church, we must begin with the progression of that person's journey. As described previously, this person experiences God's preparatory work (phase one), and receives a call from the Lord to reach a new goal (in this case a new ministry idea). Having accepted the goal (phase two), the person either by himself or herself or through intermediaries (such as leadership) seeks to include the church in the ministry (phase three).

In so doing, he/she usually discovers (and is often surprised) that others in the church have independently experienced God's call to journey along the same or similar path. Such a development serves two functions. First, this allows the ministry to become a team effort (phase two in the church's journey). Secondly, it provides objective confirmation that God's will in this specific area has been discerned accurately. It is extremely unwise to move ahead in phase three until such independent affirmation has been experienced.

As the ministry initiator links his or her journey with that of the larger church, and as the new ministry idea begins to unfold and is communicated to the congregation at large, the journey of the ministry initiator and his or her team becomes linked to the journeys of other people who may benefit from the new ministry. The church acts as a mediator in this process. This serves to draw both ministers and beneficiaries into the spiritual journey of the church at large and thus enhances and epitomizes the unity of the fellowship and the connectedness of all of our journeys in Christ. The congregation's life becomes the visible celebration of the interplay between individual spiritual journeys. Through its worship services, ministry activities, fellowship groups and celebrations, the church manifests the links that bind us together as a journeying people, signifying that the Holy Spirit is present and active within the fellowship of the faithful.

Small Group Journeys and
the Church Community

Links also exist between the journeys of small groups and the wider church fellowship. The key is to discern the theme of the group's spiritual journey, and to link it to the theme of one of the church's journeys.

The spiritual journey of small groups may be related to the church's journey in the same way that individual journeys are connected or linked to the church's journey. Each small group within a church contributes to the church's larger journey by serving as a context for spiritual journey experience and creative relational interaction between church members. A small group relates to a congregation's journey by either serving to mediate new calls that change the course of the congregation's journey, or by serving as the actual ministry expression of part of a congregation's overall journey.

When a small group's spiritual journey is not linked to the journey of the congregation at large, or when the link becomes tenuous, the small group's journey may become sidetracked. The group may begin to see itself as independent of the church fellowship, and disassociate itself from the church, or act as a potentially divisive clique. The lack of linkage between a small group and its congregation places limits on the spiritual journeys of both entities.

Journeys depend to a great extent on the relationships between people that God brings together. When such links are not encouraged, spiritual journeys are impoverished and the possibility of reaching ministry goals diminishes. The lack of linkage between the journeys of a small group and the congregation may prevent someone who should be in that group from joining it. It might also prevent the small group from changing the lives of people who are not a part of the group.

Such challenges remind us of the need to be focused and intentional as the church seeks to fulfill God's will. They also highlight the need for visionary and discerning spiritual leadership. We will turn our attention to these matters in the next chapter.

Chapter Four

Spiritual Journey-Based Church Life

"I Love the Church, but..."

I love the church, but I'm saddened by how it often fails to fulfill its call!

Faced with continual pressure to develop programs, create budgets, and attract new members, all while maintaining a level of satisfaction among those already committed to the church, many churches fail to consider the spiritual journey implications of the decisions they make regarding church life and ministry. The question of "What is God calling us to do in the future?" often takes a back seat to the following considerations:

"What did we do last year?"

"Who can we get to volunteer to do project X this year?"

"What do I want to do?"

"How do we entice others to raise their donation?"

Failing to give proper consideration to the spiritual journeys of its members, small groups and fellowship as a whole can lead to a paradoxical situation in which a church proclaims God's reality theologically while denying His living presence and lordship through its actions. We are tempted to substitute brainstorming for prayer, tradition for openness to new possibilities, volunteerism for servanthood, and human skill for God's power.

Unless we adopt a model to understand the church's spiritual journeys, there will always be the temptation to discount our dependency on God's guidance as we plan. This is not a theoretical or polemical concern, for anyone who is intimately acquainted with church life recognizes that many of our meetings, activities and programs could function even if there were no God.

Further, when a congregation does not analyze its ministries and activities according to a spiritual journey paradigm, it faces a greater possibility of becoming an institution which is more inclined to keep its members content by not rocking the boat than to receiving a prophetic call from God. Functioning more like a club than a community of journeyers who are on the move in excited response to God's vision, this type of congregation relies heavily on the extraordinary commitment and talent of a few lay leaders and the pastoral staff (who often suffer burn-out) instead of expecting all of its people to be actively engaged in ministry because they have embraced personal and group journeys. It is a church that seeks to justify its mediocrity by pointing to human limitations instead of trusting God to guide it into new spiritual journeys and to empower it so that the journeys may be successfully completed.

How easy it is for a church to lose touch with how God wishes to be active in the lives of its members! Lacking a paradigm with the spiritual resources necessary to discover God's will and presence in its corporate life, many churches uncritically hope that God's will can be equated with what the majority of the members want. Although this democratic polity option seeks to actualize the notion of the priesthood of all believers, it is blind to the fact that within every church, some people are better able to discern God's will than others. It may also lead to factionalism in the church, as people with varying desires and visions compete for influence and power within the fellowship.

This democratic option also de-emphasizes the role of the pastor as a spiritual guide who can help the church discover God's will. When important decisions are being made about the church's journey, the pastor becomes just another church member who is merely better theologically trained. His or her discernment of God's will is considered no more weighty than other opinions.

Since pastors are not expected to be spiritual guides, churches in search of a new pastor often value pleasant personalities, entertaining preaching styles, and pastoral service which emphasizes visits to homes, nursing facilities and hospitals. Rarely is a pastor asked how he/she discerns God's presence and will in his/her life and in the lives of others. Seminary education and the development of empathic skills replace spiritual discernment, wisdom and maturity in his/her pastoral ministry. Pastoral ministry becomes defined as caring for the needs of parishioners instead of leading them into sacrificial and risky service in response to God's initiative (the latter being reserved for a tiny minority of "gifted" people).

Discovering and Fulfilling God's Will

The Goal-Oriented Spiritual Journey Paradigm enables a congregation to discover and affirm God's presence in its experience. It supplies a descriptive language that is easy to learn and a spiritual framework which assures a church that God is actively involved in its journey. Most importantly, it requires that the church see itself as God's servant who must respond to His call in order to fulfill His will. It places God firmly back in control of the congregation's decision-making process and spiritual journey experience.

Furthermore, the Goal-Oriented Spiritual Journey Paradigm's analysis provides a congregation with a way of discerning God's call and validating new ministries. It is especially useful in helping the church discern God's will when there are a multiplicity of apparently good ministry opportunities available. How does a church decide on which option to accept and which to reject when they all seem like good ideas?

The Goal-Oriented Spiritual Journey Paradigm directs a church in evaluating potential ministry options by emphasizing that a ministry may only be undertaken when people within the church can testify that they have a call from God to do the ministry and that they possess the necessary life experience and spiritual gifts to fulfill the journey. According to the paradigm, a church should not undertake a new ministry, no matter how appealing or exciting it may seem, unless the requisite call has been received and affirmed by the congregation.

As with individuals, churches that are able to articulate and understand their spiritual journeys have the potential to become more confident and focused in discerning God's will. By providing concepts and language that can help us discover God's direction in our lives, the Goal-Oriented Spiritual Journey Paradigm enables parishioners to understand why someone else feels that God is leading them towards a certain goal. When a group of people can affirm that they sense a call to ministry, enthusiasm and excitement naturally result. When an individual responds to God's call to enter into a ministry journey and receives affirmation from the group, a sense of spiritual vitality and purpose emerges. When a church's activities are based on the reception of a journey call instead of on what volunteers would like to do, it becomes possible to affirm another person's ministry wholeheartedly even if we have no personal interest in or commitment to the project.

The Pastor as Spiritual Journey Director

Throughout my pastoral ministry, I have known long-time church members who have a solid knowledge of doctrine and have developed mature relationships with other members of the church, but who are unable to articulate the progression of their personal relationship with God. Even though they can testify that they have accepted Christ as Lord and Savior, they evidence a poverty of spiritual experience. They can recall few if any encounters with God as a living and personal Being who is involved in an ongoing relationship with them.

Others can point to such experiences, but are unable to articulate how such experiences are related to one another, or more generally, whether or not their spiritual journeys and encounters are coherent or purposeful. Even when they can recall a spiritual encounter with God, they often can not discern its significance and relationship to their overall spiritual life. Even more sadly, a few can "boast" of a great deal of experience that has harmed rather than helped them grow in faith, as they faced one spiritual dead end after another. Such people deserve a better and more positive encounter with the spiritual realm, and with spirituality.

A pastor's calling encompasses more than preaching, teaching, visiting, shepherding and serving as a positive role model of spiritual maturity. It also involves providing spiritual guidance and direction for people who desire to journey toward the goals that God has ordained for them and for their church. Nelson S. T. Thayer sees the pastor as a spiritual director who assists parishioners in negotiating their journey experiences:

The pastor is a guide, both for the community as a whole and for the families and individuals who constitute the congregation. The image of guide is not drawn from the context of a tour on which there are specific sights to be pointed out and explained by the guide. Rather, the image of guide is drawn from that of guiding on an arduous journey, one that includes real danger and requires rigorous attention and commitment, but also promises great beauty, depths of satisfaction, intense enjoyment, wonder, and feelings of accomplishment and deep companionship.[1]

As a spiritual guide, a pastor ministers not only in reaction to illness or crisis, but also in anticipation of spiritual growth and service. Henri Nouwen writes:

Ministers, as living reminders of Jesus Christ, are not only healers and sustainers, but also guides. The memory that heals the wounds of our past and sustains us in the present also guides us to the future and makes our lives continuously new. To be living reminders means to be prophets who, by reminding, point their people in a new direction and guide them into unknown territory.[2]

The prophetic aspect of spiritual direction requires that a pastoral guide be able to discern the difference between God's presence and the presence of evil in a person's life:

Many ministers today are excellent preachers, competent counselors, and good program administrators, but few feel comfortable giving spiritual direction to people who are searching for God's presence in their lives. For many ministers, if not for most, the life of the Holy Spirit is unknown territory. It is not surprising, therefore, that many unholy spirits have taken over and created considerable havoc. There is an increasing need for diagnosticians of the soul who can distinguish the Holy Spirit from the unholy spirits and so guide people to an active and vital transformation of soul and body, and of all their personal relationships.[3]

Thayer accepts Nouwen's assertion that spiritual discernment is vital to the role of the pastoral director. Discernment is necessary not just to root out evil, but also to make sense of positive spiritual journey experiences. All of a person's spiritual experience must be tested and interpreted in light of Christian truth:

> The point is that the contemporary pastor ministers in a time and to a congregation in which some may adopt transcendence exclusively to very narrow conservative Protestant categories; others experience themselves as having lost all capacity for the experience of transcendence; others may be open to many varieties of transcendent experience but not be able to relate them coherently to the symbols of Christian faith. Amidst such diversity the pastor must recognize, point to, facilitate, and interpret moments of the experience of transcendence.[4]

Spiritual direction furthers the process of *spiritual formation*, the deepening of our continuing relationship with God. Our people need training in the disciplines of personal and corporate prayer, silence, solitude, Bible study, fasting, and journaling. Accordingly, the providing of spiritual direction in order to further the spiritual formation of church members should be a central concern of pastoral ministry. Kenneth Leech states, "Spiritual direction therefore is not a fringe activity, a 'specialized' form of ministry (although there will be specialists here as in other areas), but it is an integral part of the ordinary pastoral work to which every priest is called."[5]

As important as spiritual formation is, it is not an end in itself. The church develops the spiritual lives of its people *so that they may serve God more effectively by ministering to others in the world.* Thus, another goal of spiritual direction is to enable individuals and churches to anticipate (phase one), discern and embrace (phase two), fulfill (phase three) and celebrate and learn from (phase four) their spiritual journeys. Spiritual direction, as a pastoral ministry, is an effort to intentionally promote and facilitate progress in the spiritual journeys of our members and congregations. In fulfilling such a role, the pastor must be attuned to the voice of God and be able to discern the course of the spiritual journeys taking place within the church.

Being attentive to the voice of God while discerning the course of spiritual journeys, both individual and corporate, requires spiritual guides and leaders to be excellent *listeners*. We must listen not just to the inner voice which (we hope) comes from God, but also to the messages emanating from the journeys of the people we are directing. Taken as a whole, these messages represent the voice of God.

Pastors can guide congregations only to the extent that they listen to the themes and wisdom which the many journeys express. It's like listening to a symphony which God has composed, with each journey representing an instrumental part. It is not sufficient to listen to only some of the journeys, which is a common mistake. When we hear all of the journeys, each in their proper place, previously undiscovered links between the journeys and grand themes emerge which provide the beauty and majesty of the complex composition which we call the life of the church. While the task of most parishioners is to play out their specific journeys, the unique responsibility of the pastor as spiritual director is to serve as a conductor who hears and directs the entire spiritual performance.

Pastors must also exercise discernment in regard to facilitating a proper relationship between individual and corporate redemptive and mission-level journeys. There are four considerations that we need to bear in mind in this regard.

First, spiritual direction and pastoral care should guide people and churches through redemptive journeys so that God may call them to mission-level experiences. Pastors must not be satisfied with permitting parishioners to go endlessly from one redemptive spiritual journey to another, which encourages self-centeredness. Parishioners must come to understand that God gives them healing, spiritual knowledge and fulfilling relationships for more than just their own welfare or benefit. Such gifts, if they are to reach their full potential, must be given away to others through mission and service.

Therefore, our pastoral interest in peoples' lives must lead them to view the ending of a redemptive journey not as a conclusion of our shepherding task, but rather as a milestone which serves to remind all concerned that God has been preparing the journeyers for mission. A redemptive journey should be understood as a phase one experience for a mission journey.

Second, it is a serious mistake to force a mission journey on people who presently need to experience a redemptive journey. Pastors and church leaders must exercise discernment in this area to avoid discouraging and harming potential journeyers. People who are hurting and in need of healing will often express their anguish over being stuck in phase one of a mission journey. They have no ministry direction and no goal to journey toward, and this is sometimes a symptom of a need to deal with a redemptive journey issue. Since a redemptive journey is foundational to future mission experiences, such people should be encouraged to make the redemptive journey a priority, and to move on to a mission journey at a later time. Redemptive needs and issues take precedence over mission concerns in terms of spiritual guidance.

Third, pastors and church leaders should take the redemptive/mission level distinction into account as they guide the formation of small groups within the church. Small groups which focus on relational, healing and spiritual growth issues are concerned with redemptive journeys. As such, they contribute to the church's overall journey by strengthening their members' inner spiritual experience. However, redemptive small groups also should feed into the larger journey of the church by serving as ministry initiators (emerging out of the growth experiences of the members of the group), and by enabling and challenging group members to move on to mission journeys when God calls them. Pastoral leadership should encourage the emergence of mission journeys as a necessary and positive fruit of redemptive group experiences.

Fourth, in some denominations, the so-called "interim period" between pastorates should be understood as a redemptive spiritual journey, which has been sequenced between two mission journeys. It is not merely a marker of the time between the going and coming of a pastor, but a self-contained spiritual journey in its own right. Not only does it serve as phase five of the just-concluded mission journey and phase one of the anticipated near-future mission journey which will commence with the call of a new minister, but in and of itself, it represents the church's need for periodic corporate times of healing, introspection and renewal. An interim period is the sabbath rest of a congregation, denoting not inactivity, but a time of refocusing. It is not something to be impatient with. A "let's get this over with as soon as possible" mentality is often quite destructive to a church and misses the point of the journey.

From a spiritual journey perspective, the interim period journey of the church does not end solely with the calling of a new pastor, but also with the congregation completing its own redemptive/learning experience. The success of the next pastorate and mission journey can be decisively influenced by the congregation's willingness to embrace and patiently fulfill its redemptive journey. If it does not do so, it will condemn itself to repeating mistakes of the past or bringing past hurts which remain unhealed into the new journey.

Spiritual Journey-Based Ministry

Imagine what church life would look and feel like if we intentionally based it on the principles and values of the Goal-Oriented Spiritual Journey Paradigm! A church which values and promotes spiritual journeying as the central metaphor of congregational life will find that the paradigm can be applied to all aspects of its ministry to its members and the world. In the following pages, I will share one way to visualize that application. It is by no means the only way, and I would encourage the reader to let his or her imagination run wild in creating different scenarios based on the circumstances unique to his or her situation.

Spiritual Journey-Based Evangelism

I have probably experienced just about every method of evangelism the church has devised!

Park and street witnessing to strangers, evangelistic book tables and literature distribution in major metropolitan transportation terminals, coffee house evangelism, house-to-house evangelism explosion, invite-a-friend to church services, two Billy Graham mass evangelism crusades, small group home meetings and inductive Bible studies, felt-need outreaches, mass-mailings of evangelistic newspapers, power evangelism, and sharing the gospel through the media (over radio, t.v. and the internet) are just some of the ways I've attempted to share my faith in Christ. And, yes, I've even used the four spiritual laws! For years, I've shared the good news from the pulpits of churches, and spent countless hours privately speaking with spiritual seekers.

69

What have I gleaned from all of this evangelistic experience? Virtually any method can be used by God to enable people to manifest faith in Christ, and no method has the power to convince all kinds of people that they should convert. There is no one Biblical method to effectively communicate the timeless truths of the gospel. No method can force people against their will into the kingdom of God, and some people enter the kingdom with no evangelistic method even being employed (I converted to Christ, for example, without anyone sharing the gospel with me). People saw Jesus perform miracles and didn't convert, while Paul converts without having a Peter preach to him (though the latter does a great job with Cornelius). We prefer using some methods over others, while our hearers are predisposed to respond more favorably to particular methods, based on personality and circumstances.

Personality and circumstances. These two words bring us back to spiritual journeying, for in our attempts to share good news we must remember that we are dealing with people who are journeying through life with varying degrees of awareness about God, themselves and their spiritual life. We cannot ignore or discount *their* experience as we share *our* message. Accordingly, *our evangelism must be spiritual journey-based*.

Spiritual journey-based evangelism *respects the integrity of peoples' spiritual journeys*. *Respect* does not mean uncritical acceptance of journeys whose themes run counter to God's values, since not all journeys are equally expressive of God's will (as the next chapter will demonstrate). I am also not saying that all religions are valid paths to God. Instead, respecting the integrity of peoples' spiritual journeys involves listening to their stories with an open and discerning heart in order to discover the hidden hand of God at work in their lives. Respect prevents us from asking for inappropriate responses or concentrating on irrelevant issues. Every journey hints at God's plan and dreams for our lives. The true evangelist, so well exemplified by Jesus when he speaks with Nicodemus in the dark of night and with the woman at the well who hides the true facts of her experience out of shame (John 3-4), listens for the deep themes in a person's life in order to help the person embrace God's will.

Respecting the integrity of journeys also means that we do not rush or hinder a journey's progress. Rather than trying to coerce people

70

into premature decisions which they may not be ready to make or understand, we should seriously consider what peoples' journeys are really telling us about their spiritual needs and awareness, and respond accordingly. It also means that we resolve to use only those evangelistic methods which are compatible with the journey we are seeking to influence. Spiritual journey-based evangelism is not wedded, either in practice or in theory, to a particular methodology.

Spiritual journey-based evangelism *challenges people to further their journeys, supports their efforts to grow spiritually, and encourages them to see themselves as spiritual beings.* Our role as evangelists is to encourage people to journey closer to God, and the more we understand the dynamics of their journeys, the better able we will be to exert a positive influence. With confidence in the Holy Spirit's ability to lead journeyers toward the light of Christ (phase one), we seek to help them acknowledge on a conscious level Jesus as the Lord of their journeys (phase two) and to follow Him as committed disciples (phase three).

Depending on how far a potential believer's journey has progressed, the most appropriate response at a given moment may not be proclaiming but listening empathetically; at other times, explicitly sharing the gospel may be appropriate. Timing is everything in influencing the course of a journey, and we must be very sensitive to when and how we share. All too often, we needlessly turn people off to a faith-inspired life because we have presented the good news at an inappropriate time, without regard to who our listeners are and where their journeys have taken them thus far.

Spiritual journey-based evangelism does not see conversion as the end of a process, but rather as the initiation of a discipleship process in which the new believer will be challenged by God and the church to embrace many new spiritual journeys. It's just the beginning!

Spiritual Journey-Based Discipleship

I never attended Sunday School until I was seventeen years old because I was raised in a Jewish home (I never had the privilege of attending the synagogue's classes for children, either). My interest in the Scriptures and Christian teachings stemmed from the dynamics

71

of a journey which began with a powerful mystical experience when I converted to Christ at age fourteen. From then until the beginning of my studies at a Christian college at age eighteen, I read through the entire Bible more than half a dozen times and devoured scores of Christian books. In order to further the journey, I needed knowledge and wisdom, and was thus motivated to search for it.

When I entered college, I naively thought that I would be far behind other students in my understanding and application of Christianity because they had attended church all of their lives. Much to my surprise and disillusionment, I discovered the opposite was the case. Most of my peers, in spite of enduring more than 15 years of Sunday School, church services, and youth groups, had never read through the Gospels, let alone the rest of the Scriptures. Few manifested much understanding of the message of the sacred texts in spite of knowing the story outlines of Noah, David and Goliath and Jonah. After almost two decades of being spoon-fed "flannel graph" Christianity, not many appeared to be actively seeking growth in their spiritual lives. It was like pulling teeth to recruit volunteers for on-campus prayer and outreach activities.

Being "raised in the church" did little for most of my peers' spiritual life, whereas the journeys I experienced as a teenager powerfully motivated me to grow as a young Christian. Was not being raised in church advantageous for my spiritual growth?

Is there anyone who truly believes that the current way our churches disciple youth and adults can overcome the influence secular society has over their hearts, minds and spirituality? How can a classroom-based one or two hour exposure to the Christian life (a Sunday School class plus a midweek youth group or Bible study) be as engrossing as the modern culture which calls to us through the mass media (television, movies, radio, music), the school system and the myriads of sporting and career opportunities?

For too long the contemporary church has hid its head in the sand as we lose new generations of "church kids" to non-Christian lifestyles and allegiances. Children look upon confirmation or baptism (at around age 13) as the graduation *from* attending religious instruction rather than as a milestone in which they make the transition from childhood faith to mature faith. Is it any wonder that many, if not most, adults approach the Bible and their responsibilities as a member of the community of faith with no more sophistication or insight than that of a child?

Discipleship takes place in light of and in response to peoples' journeys, and its goal must be to further those journeys.

Journeys provide the life context in which our true needs, hopes and dreams emerge as we respond to God's will. This is why we hold new members classes, create specialized support groups, and segregate people into age-based programs. However, such efforts sometimes miss the point because labeling people and their needs, hopes or comfort zones is not synonymous with discerning the theme of their individual spiritual journeys.

A spiritual journey-based discipleship process listens to the person (or group) who is journeying in order to discern the theme and nature of the journeys which have been completed and to discover what journeys are currently in progress. Following such an analysis, the church offers whatever resources it possessed to support the progress of the journey(s). This might include the creation of a new class, the invitation to one which already exists, or one-on-one mentoring by someone who has prior experience with the theme of the journey.

Whatever the response, the key point is this: the goal of discipling is the faithful fulfillment of journeys. Spiritual growth is not determined by statistical measurements like class attendance (since attendance does not equal learning) or even graduation from one age level class to the next (for no one gets left back in church school!), but by whether both the discipler and the disciple can attest to the progression of the journey.

Spiritual journey-based discipleship, therefore, requires students to accept a high degree of personal responsibility. They have to engage in a continual reflection process in order to gain self-understanding and to consciously own the journey(s) which determine the course of their spiritual lives. They have to commit themselves to growing spiritually so that their journeys will be fulfilled.

The church fellowship, in turn, must also accept a higher level of responsibility, for it commits itself to be flexible and open in nurturing the journey process of its members. Working together, disciples and church fellowship become accountable to one another, for both must be faithful if the journeys are to be completed.

This approach implies the need for *an individualized spiritual journey plan* for those who seek to further their journeys in an intentional manner. Whether formal or informal, such a plan would chart the course of one's journey according to the phases of the Goal-Oriented Spiritual Journey Paradigm. The plan represents the understanding between those journeying and their mentors concerning the nature and course of the journeys and specifically how both will commit themselves to furthering those journeys. As the journeys progress, and as new ones emerge, the plan (acting like a spiritual journal) would be revised.

Promoting such intentionality in charting journey progress as part of the discipleship ministry of the church encourages the active participation of key players and helps people focus their energies wisely. It also provides a new way to celebrate spiritual growth in our lives, especially when journeys come to a conclusion.

Spiritual journey-based discipleship encourages links between the corporate journey of the congregation and the individual journeys of its members. As members mature and develop spiritual gifts, the corporate journey provides a context in which those gifts can be explored and practiced. As relationships begin and blossom, people find partners whose journeys are linked to their own. The life of the fellowship gives birth to new journeys, nurtures them and celebrates their completion, and in turn, individual journeys enhance and further the corporate journey.

Spiritual Journey-Based Worship and Preaching

A church's corporate spiritual journey is celebrated and articulated during times of gathering together as a fellowship of faith. The celebration takes place in and through our worship, and the articulation of the journey takes place in a significant way through preaching.

A great divide exists between traditionalists and advocates of contemporary praise or seeker-sensitive worship styles. Both camps have significant points to make in the debate, but to my mind, the debate itself is beside the point.

A particular style of worship is not prescribed in the Scriptures, and therefore presumably we are free to invent worship styles based on Christian values, group taste and culture. Experience teaches us that the presence of God is able to permeate varied forms of worship. In light of this, mature Christians, although personally preferring certain styles, should be able to appreciate other styles, and if necessary, be able to experience God through such styles. The cultural and ethnic diversity of the contemporary Christian scene cries out for such flexibility and maturity.

Our worship services should be spiritually journey-based. Regardless of what style of worship a church embraces, our worship services should authentically reflect the journeys of the church, both past and present. Paul defines worship, not as an event, but as an act of supreme submission to the Lord of the journey:

> Therefore, I urge you, brothers, in view of God's mercy, to offer your bodies as living sacrifices, holy and pleasing to God - this is your spiritual act of worship. Do not conform any longer to the pattern of this world, but be transformed by the renewing of your mind. Then you will be able to test and approve what God's will is - his good, pleasing and perfect will. (Romans 12:1-2)

Our spiritual act of worship is to give ourselves totally (body and mind) to God so that we will be able to do His will. In other words, worshipping God is implicitly equated with fulfilling our spiritual journeys. Corporate worship in praise, song and prayer (and even the taking of offerings!) should reflect this orientation toward God. There is no authenticity in a worship service that celebrates our allegiance to God if such commitment is not reflected in the living out of our journeys outside of the worship time!

One of the ways in which we have sought to express this principle at my church is to revive the sharing of lay testimonies in modified form. The rehearsing and celebrating of spiritual experience has been a vital part of worship since the Exodus, and was central to Jewish temple worship. However, in many churches, testimonies are limited to conversion experiences which often took place decades ago, giving the impression that one's personal relationship with God after

75

conversion is inconsequential. In our lay testimonies at First Baptist, Lincoln, people are invited to share specific journeys which are either recently completed or still ongoing. Beyond the telling of a story, the testimonies contain a good amount of reflection on the journey's significance. Such commentary is concerned with how each phase of the journey has been experienced, how God's grace has been manifested along the way, and what the person has learned because of the journey.

Spiritual journey-based worship needs to be supported by spiritual journey-based preaching. Spiritual journey-based preaching involves the preparation and delivery of Biblically-based pastoral messages which articulate, clarify, encourage and foster the spiritual journeys of the church. Such messages address the concerns raised by the individual and corporate spiritual journeys of the congregation, sometimes in a necessarily prophetic manner.

Examples of such sermons abound in the Scriptures. The prophets spoke forcefully and directly, not about theoretical religious or philosophical issues, but about the extent to which Israel was either succeeding in fulfilling its God-given journey, or more often, failing to live out its journey faithfully. Jesus' messages had the same prophetic quality, and the Sermon on the Mount (Matthew 5-7) is obviously focused on furthering spiritual journeys.

A spiritual journey-based understanding of preaching impacts how I select texts and themes for my messages. In some traditions, the text and theme is given to the preacher. In other traditions, the preacher is free to choose. How one chooses is an interesting process; among the many texts, themes, issues and doctrines yearning for our attention, how do we choose one instead of another?

Spiritual journey-based preaching requires that the decision be made in light of the needs and demands of the spiritual journeys of the congregation. My sermons must speak to the journeys, and so before I can even select a text or message theme, I first must identify and analyze the church's spiritual journeys according to the Goal-Oriented Spiritual Journey Paradigm. I consider the journey themes, and then prepare messages which will enhance the ability of the congregation to grasp, affirm, and fulfill their journeys.

Spiritual journey-based preaching, like the revised form of lay testimony mentioned above, assumes that the speaker has experience with the journey and its theme, and thus can reflect on it from a personal perspective. In his sermon to Cornelius' household, Peter makes it clear that he personally witnessed Jesus' life, ministry and death (Acts 10:39). In one of the letters attributed to him, Peter says, "We did not follow cleverly invented stories when we told you about the power and coming of our Lord Jesus Christ, but we were eyewitnesses of his majesty" (2 Peter 1:16).

Similarly, John states, "That which was from the beginning, which we have heard, which we have seen with our eyes, which we have looked at and our hands have touched - this we proclaim concerning the Word of life" (1 John 1:1). Wisdom results from the processing of human journey experience in light of God's word, and this is what we should pass on to those who come to church each Sunday seeking spiritual nourishment.

A speaker's personal journey experience serves an essential role in authenticating the message. The writer to the Hebrews advises, "Remember your leaders, who spoke the word of God to you. Consider the outcome of their way of life and imitate their faith" (Hebrews 13:7). Whenever I take a trip, I seek the advice of experienced travelers who have been to the place I am going, but pay little attention to advice provided by inexperienced travelers who have not visited my destination. Pastors are on sure ground when their sermon points have been authenticated by their personal spiritual journey experience; as spiritual guides, we are to lead people along paths we have traveled in order to facilitate their journeys. Preaching about issues we have no personal experience of at best produces shallow advice and at worst can lead people into journey difficulties.

Worship and preaching are inseparably tied together. Listening to God's word preached in order to gain insight into one's journey is just as much worship as singing praise choruses. If Paul is right in Romans 12:1-3, then worship is only pleasing to God when it symbolizes *complete obedience* to living out God's will. You can sing as many songs as you like and feel all kinds of positive emotions, but if at the same time you are not committed to your journey and seeking God's will, you haven't worshipped!

77

By preaching messages which facilitate the progress of a church's spiritual journeys, pastors serve as "shepherds of God's flock" (1 Peter 5:2). As a shepherd guides a flock and moves them along, so too a pastor is entrusted with the responsibility of moving his or her flock along the journey path toward God's will. This naturally leads us to our next concern - spiritual journey-based administration.

Spiritual Journey-Based Administration

Determining and then helping a church fulfill God's will is the fundamental task of administration. In the previous chapter, the steps of administering the acceptance of a journey vision were detailed. It is the responsibility of the pastor, the journey mediator and the lay leadership of a church to facilitate the church's reception, acceptance and fulfillment of spiritual journeys, and to encourage the wedding of peoples' spiritual gifts to those journeys. Strategic issues and program options should always be explored in light of the church's past and present spiritual journeys, and in light of future journey possibilities.

How do we discern God's will when we stand before a possible open door of opportunity and service? Following are some principles which I employ as I seek God's will and encourage my church to fulfill its journeys.

First, only those journeys which conform to the values, principles and characteristics of God, as revealed in the Bible, may be affirmed as God's will. Journeys that embody God's will challenge us, both individually and collectively, to draw closer to God and be more conformed to His image (Eph. 1:15-23; 3:17-19; 1 Thess. 4:3-10). A journey that expresses God's will challenges us as a community of faith to manifest His presence in a more faithful way.

Second, we should always distinguish between our personal interests, likes and dislikes, and the will of God. God is free to challenge His people with an agenda for mission that may or may not correspond to one's personal feelings or opinions. Some Biblical examples include: God calls Jonah to prophesy mercy to Nineveh even though Jonah does not want to go to save his enemies, and God calls Peter to preach to Cornelius - a Gentile - even though Peter is at first resistant to the notion. Journeys often challenge us to transcend our own feelings so that we may grow in Christ and in faithfulness.

78

Third, a journey that calls for us to change course often inspires conflicting emotions in us, both positive and negative, such as: awe, excitement, hope, fear, anger, insecurity, and resistance. Our response often, therefore, tells us more about ourselves than about the vision's viability. When we experience such emotions, we should search for the roots of the feelings before allowing the feelings to inform our decision regarding the journey.

Fourth, a journey, when presented to a church, will often test our ability to trust and submit to one another (especially our leadership), to embrace risk, and to exercise faith. This is especially true when the journey has been mediated by someone other than ourselves. Issues of jealousy, ego, pride and status come into play when God calls us to accept a journey mediated through another person, and we must resist such negative powers as we seek God's will. It does not matter who initially receives a journey vision. How often we say we want pastors to be "strong leaders" - but we can be so resistant to following, obeying and submitting to that leadership (note Heb. 13:17). I am not asserting that pastors are perfect or that lay people should be mindless followers, but responsible thinking, reflection and prayer should be wedded to trust and faith in our leaders.

Fifth, when we are called to embrace a journey, we should be able to testify concerning our phase one preparation. We should be able to demonstrate that we already have the necessary talents and spiritual gifts demanded by the journey, or sense that God is giving us new gifts in light of the call. If we do not posses such gifts, we should be able to show how our journey has been linked to another person's journey who will be able to minister in a complementary and cooperative fashion with us in order to fulfill the journey goal.

If a journey passes all of the above tests, we should ask God directly if the journey is His will. In general, there are five possible answers God gives in response to a phase two prayer for guidance:

1. *Yes.* If this is the reply, then we should embrace the journey as faithfully as possible by moving on to phase three.

2. *Yes, but the timing is not right or some revision is necessary.* If we sense this response, we should allow the journey vision to continue growing in us until we sense the time is right or until new insights have been gained. This is God's

way of telling us that we are really still in phase one and that we have prematurely assumed we are in phase two.

3. *No.* If the answer is no, we should learn what we can from the rejected journey but not act on the journey itself. This tells us that we are in an early stage of phase one of a journey which will probably take us in a very different direction than we had imagined.

4. *God maintains silence.* In this case, we should continue asking for definitive inner guidance and check to see if God has chosen to reply by speaking to others we trust. If they believe God has spoken to them, we give them the benefit of the doubt and trust them. God's silence usually means that phase two is not ready to be concluded.

5. *Someone else is called to that journey.* If another person claims to have a call and is credible, and God has not spoken directly to us, we should support their efforts by encouraging them to move on to phase three. We should then pray to see how God might want to link our journey to theirs.

The above observations are not to be applied legalistically, but should be utlilized as guidelines as we seek to be open to God's will. If the journey really isn't God's will, such openness will allow God to correct one's course. Faith and risk-taking are certainly part of the process, and can never be eliminated by rational processes. However, embracing a journey by faith is worth the risk, for if a prospective journey is never entered into, a positive outcome is impossible.

Spiritual Journey-Based Mission

The most important goal-oriented spiritual journey Jesus has called the Christian church to embrace is the Great Commission (Matthew 28:16-20). As Lord of the journey ("all authority in heaven and on earth has been given to me"), Jesus promises His abiding presence throughout the journey ("I am with you always") and lays out the journey goal: "go and make disciples of all nations, baptizing them in the name of the Father and of the Son and of the Holy Spirit, and teaching them to obey everything I have commanded you." We journey to the nations so that people everywhere may embrace Jesus as

Lord and hear His call to journey for the sake of the kingdom. *Mission is the primary spiritual journey of God's people!*

Spiritual journey-based mission endorses the notion that every Christian is in some sense a missionary. This obviously does not mean that everyone is called to be a career missionary any more than the doctrine of the priesthood of all believers means that everyone is called to be a pastor. Nor does it do away with those specialized journeys. Rather, spiritual journey-based mission implies that throughout one's life, God calls us serve the Kingdom through specific short or long-term goal-oriented journeys whose themes relate to the great commission mandate.

These mission-centered spiritual journeys should not be limited in variety. Under the umbrella of this form of journey are the vocational careers of a long-term international missionaries, the short-term missions project, social action outreaches, health-related ministries, evangelism of all sizes and methods, etc. The destructive ideologically-based antithesis between traditional evangelism and social action in missions (and local church life) is false. The Kingdom of God is large enough to embrace both at the same time, and there are enough people within the Kingdom to hear God's call to journey in both areas to ensure that their agendas are completely fulfilled.

The problem really is not that one form of witness detracts from the other but that too many people do not choose to heed God's call in either area. *We need to help people recognize, embrace and fulfill their mission-centered spiritual journeys* instead of permitting them to believe that being "missions-minded" means simply giving money so that others can do the work. Jesus' words are as true now as they were when he first shared them with his disciples: "The harvest is plentiful but the workers are few. As the Lord of the harvest, therefore, to send out workers into his harvest field" (Matthew 9:37-38).

The message we proclaim to the nations must be spiritual journey-based. Why is it that Christianity has not become the majority religion in any region of the world where another major religion first reigned? Early Christianity's evangelical message, with its emphasis on holiness as pleasing to a righteous yet forgiving God who does not act arbitrarily, was sufficient to render less morally-based religions (such as the ancient Roman and animist faiths)

81

obsolete. However, Judaism, Islam, Hinduism, Buddhism, Taoism, and Confucianism (the other six major world religions) embody a vision of holiness that is as deep as Christianity's, while also, each in their own way, offering a coherent and sophisticated spiritual journey paradigm which makes experience *meaningful* for their adherents.

Until contemporary Christianity boldly weds its evangelical doctrinal message to a coherent spiritual journey paradigm which makes experience richer for people of other faiths, it will not be able to claim spiritual victory over them or gain a significant number of converts from among their ranks of serious adherents. The creative re-integration of a spiritual journey paradigm into our conversation with other religions is one of the most important missiological tasks confronting the church in the twenty-first century. If we do not accomplish this, other religions will continue to grow stronger in traditionally Christian areas such as Europe and North America, continuing a trend we see taking place at the present time.

Chapter Five

When Spiritual Journeys Go Astray

The Impact of Sin and Unfaithfulness
on Spiritual Journeys

In a perfect world, the five phases of our goal-oriented spiritual journeys would proceed without any hindrances. Progress towards God's goals for our lives would be smooth and steady, and no opposition would be experienced. Every journey inevitably would reach its appointed phase four conclusion, and we would experience the joy of resurrection and the broadening horizons of ever more challenging future journeys.

Unfortunately, it is painfully obvious that we do not live in a perfect world and that our spiritual journeys do not always progress toward their conclusion without opposition, problems, delays and detours. The presence of sin, defined as unfaithfulness to God and others, in our personal lives and in the world, allied with our God-given ability to exercise free will, often plays a decisively negative role in spiritual journeys. We must never minimize the adverse impact of evil as we journey. Sin and evil do hinder and derail spiritual journeys, as the following Biblical journeys illustrate.

Adam and Eve in the Garden:
A Journey Ends in Failure

The Genesis stories chronicle the spiritual journeys of people who were among the first humans to encounter the revelatory presence of God. The creation story involving Adam and Eve in the Garden of Eden (Genesis 1-3), for example, portrays a journey which self-destructs in phase three, with disastrous consequences for humanity.

Genesis 1:1-25 and 2:1-14 describe the creation of the universe and this dual account represents the transpersonal phase one preparation for Adam and Eve's journey. Their phase two journey call is found in Genesis 1:26-30 and 2:15-17 and involves being responsible for creation and, implicitly, for growing in the knowledge of how they are related to the created order and to God. This call emphasizes that a person should not journey in isolation from significant relationships. At the start, Adam and Eve's journeys are linked, symbolizing the unity and faithfulness of the marital relationship (Genesis 2:18-24). In their innocence, Adam and Eve begin their spiritual journey without an awareness of sin and unfaithfulness (Genesis 2:25).

The Genesis account blames the serpent, representing Satan, for successfully enticing the inexperienced couple to disobey God by eating the forbidden fruit of the tree of the knowledge of good and evil (Genesis 3:1-7). The effect of this temptation is to create a divide between God and the two journeyers. This divide is characterized by *unfaithfulness* - a breaking of the cooperation and trust that must exist between God and us if we are to progress through phase three. Once disloyalty has usurped cooperation and distrust has replaced trust, phase three is disrupted. Alienation between God and us, and also between others and ourselves, naturally results (Genesis 3:8-13). The intrusion of sin into Adam and Eve's spiritual journey leads to judgment (Genesis 3:14-19) and the premature ending of the journey, which is symbolized by Adam and Eve being driven out of the Garden (Genesis 3:20-24).

The Tower of Babel: A Shadow Journey

Gen. 11:1-9 is a tale of a spiritual journey gone awry. It is a *shadow journey* (a journey that draws people further away from God's will) on a grand scale. As such, it serves as a warning to anyone who seeks to dethrone God as Lord of the journey.

Phase two of this journey, for example, does not begin with God calling the people of Shinar (Babylonia) to construct a city; rather, they take the initiative to decide that this is what they want to do (Gen. 11:3-4) without God's input or direction. This is why God has to symbolically "come down to see the city and the tower that the men were building" (Gen. 11:5) - He was excluded from the journey.

84

The account quickly turns to the consequences of such presumptuousness. Rather than empowering the journey, God opposes its progress by "confusing their language so they will not understand each other" (Gen. 11:7). Since phase 3 requires cooperation, loyalty and trust between journeyers, the confusing of their languages was intended to destroy their ability to cooperate with one another. Thus, from a spiritual journey perspective, common language symbolizes cooperation between journeys that have been linked together. If we don't speak "the same language" and understand one another, how can we journey together in peace and harmony?

The Exodus: A Corporate Journey
Fails to Progress

In chapter two, we outlined Moses' spiritual journey as Israel's leader during the Exodus. The Torah can also be read from the perspective of the group he led, the Israelite people, as they journey from oppression in Egypt to freedom in the Promised Land.

The Genesis account of the creation of the world by the invisible God (revealed as Yahweh in Moses' burning bush call), Abraham's journey from Ur to Canaan and his receiving of the covenant from God, Joseph's experiences in Egypt, and Israel's enslavement under the Pharaohs (Exodus 1), all serve as a phase one prelude for God's call to the Israelites to journey to a new existence. The nation's corporate phase one experience also includes its leadership experiencing its own phase two call, which is mediated by Moses and Aaron:

> Moses and Aaron brought together all the elders of the Israelites, and Aaron told them everything the LORD had said to Moses. He also performed the signs before the people, and they believed. And when they heard that the LORD was concerned about them and had seen their misery, they bowed down and worshipped. (Exodus 4:29-31)

Following Moses' confrontation with Pharaoh, the ten plagues and the first Passover experience (Exodus 5-12), phase two begins as the Jewish people leave Egypt, cross the Red Sea (Exodus 12:31-14:31), and receive the Covenant and the Law at Mt. Sinai (Exodus 19-23). At Mt. Sinai, the people are called by God to form a new society under the protection of Yahweh by traveling to a new land (the journey destination) and by living a new life (as outlined by the Mosaic Law). Phase two for the people reaches a successful conclusion when the covenant is embraced: "Then he [Moses] took the Book of the Covenant and read it to the people. They responded, 'We will do everything the LORD has said; we will obey'" (Exodus 24:7).

Phase three of Israel's corporate journey toward the Promised Land is summarized at the end of Exodus, emphasizing the cooperative relationship between Yahweh as leader and the people as followers: "In all the travels of the Israelites, whenever the cloud lifted from above the tabernacle, they would set out; but if the cloud did not lift, they did not set out - until the day it lifted. So the cloud of the LORD was over the tabernacle by day, and fire was in the cloud by night, in the sight of all the house of Israel during all their travels" (Exodus 40:36-38).

Sadly, in the book of Numbers, we discover how Israel allows sin to derail its journey toward Canaan. Throughout the journey, sin expresses itself as an unwillingness to cooperate with God and others in reaching the accepted goal of the journey. When sin is not held in check during phase three, the journeyers lose the vision which they received during phase two. Discouraged by the report from the spies, they lose the enthusiasm which is so essential to the spiritual life. They cannot receive the positive exhortation from Joshua and Caleb to journey on (Numbers 13:25-33). The people rebel against and thus refuse to cooperate with God's appointed leaders, and begin to even distrust God:

> That night all the people of the community raised their voices and wept aloud. All the Israelites grumbled against Moses and Aaron, and the whole assembly said to them, "If only we had died in Egypt! Or in this desert! Why is the LORD bringing us to this land only to let us fall by the sword? Our wives and children will be taken as plunder. Wouldn't it be better for us to go back to Egypt?" And they said to each other, "We should choose a leader and go back to Egypt." (Numbers 14:1-4)

This is not an isolated or momentary lapse of cooperation. Throughout the journey in the desert, Moses' leadership and God's goodwill are challenged and questioned by the people (such as during the quarrel at Meribah, in Numbers 20:1-13) and by other lesser

86

leaders, such as Miriam and Aaron (Numbers 12), and Korah, Dathan and Abiram (Numbers 16).

God's response to these all too frequent rebellious episodes involves not only forgiveness through an atonement for sins (Numbers 14:10-25), but also judgment. There is a price to pay for repeatedly failing to fulfill the phase three virtues of cooperation, loyalty and trust. The original generation of Jews who left Egypt only to rebel will not be permitted to reach the Promised Land; they will not be successful in reaching phase four of their spiritual journey.

Instead, the rebellious leaders will perish, and the people will wander aimlessly - as opposed to making progress towards a journey goal - throughout the desert and die without reaching their potential as God's people. Only Caleb and Joshua remain true and faithful to the journey's vision and cooperate with both God and Moses, and thus they alone from the original generation will be allowed to experience phase four by entering Canaan (Numbers 14:26-38).

In response, the community appears to repent and seek forgiveness. Nevertheless, the people betray just how ingrained their unfaithfulness is by seeking to continue the journey presumptuously, and without regard for the authority of Moses, their leader. As a result, their impetuousness leads to a military defeat, demonstrating that it is not possible to further a spiritual journey while being out of step with God and the community's leaders (Numbers 14:39-45).

Many contemporary congregations are in a similar situation without realizing it. By refusing to forge cooperative relationships with their leaders (especially their pastors), and by refusing to maintain a clear and focused sense of vision regarding the journey goals God has ordained for them, many congregations have allowed sin and unfaithfulness to disrupt their phase three experience. In judgment, God allows such congregations to wander aimlessly through a spiritual desert. Their activity blinds them to the sadness of their situation. Aimless wandering, no matter how vigorously pursued, does not contribute to the advancement of God's kingdom or to the progress of a community's journey.

As we follow the Exodus saga from Numbers to Deuteronomy, another aspect of phase three comes into focus: *since sin and unfaithfulness can so deeply disturb the course of a community's spiritual journey, God sometimes offers His people the option of covenant renewal to get us back on track.* Covenant renewal is an opportunity to "return to the LORD and obey him" in light of the revelation that he is "a merciful God" who "will not abandon or destroy his people" (Deuteronomy 4:30-31). Love and obedience go hand in hand in an authentic covenant renewal experience (Deuteronomy 6:1-9; 7:11-13; 8:6; 11:1-32).

By renewing our covenant with God, we reaffirm the call which we experienced previously in phase two, repent of the sins which have prevented us from fully cooperating with God and others in phase three, and once again set our sights on God's goals for our lives (phase four). This is precisely the opportunity presented to Israel in Deuteronomy. Deuteronomy 1-3 rehearses Israel's phase three failures in spite of God's continuing faithfulness. Israel is urged to renew her covenant with God (Deuteronomy 4), the substance of which takes up the bulk of the book (chapters 5-28). With the covenant renewed, Israel experiences a change in leadership (Joshua replaces Moses) and is poised to resume her corporate journey.

Jonah's Refusal to Embrace His Journey

What happens when we refuse to embrace a journey? Jonah's story illustrates how sin manifested in phase two can alter the course of a spiritual journey, and how sin manifested in phase four can prevent us from experiencing God's peace and satisfaction.

The opening chapter describes Jonah's initial phase two encounter with God's revelation for his life. He rejects God's call to embrace a prophetic journey for the sake of the Ninevites, and accordingly attempts to flee from God's presence so as to not be punished for his disobedience (perhaps believing that God could not harm him outside of Israel):

> The word of the LORD came to Jonah son of Amittai: "Go to the great city of Nineveh and preach against it, because its wickedness has come up before me." But Jonah ran away from the LORD and headed for Tarshish. He went down to Joppa, where he found a ship bound for that port. After paying the fare,

he went aboard and sailed for Tarshish to flee from the LORD. (Jonah 1:1-3)

The essential nature of sin during phase two is the rejection of a legitimate call to journey toward a God-ordained goal. Sinning in such a manner does not end a journey, as if accepting God's call were optional. Rather, it forces the insubordinate person to begin a rebellious shadow journey towards an alternate (but illusory) destination or goal. This is illustrated by Jonah's irrational attempt to reach Tarsus instead of Nineveh.

God judges Jonah's rebellion in order to bring about his repentance (Jonah 1:4-2:10) so that the original spiritual journey call could be repeated. This time, Jonah responds affirmatively:

Then the word of the LORD came to Jonah a second time: "Go to the great city of Nineveh and proclaim to it the message I give you." Jonah obeyed the word of the LORD and went to Nineveh. Now Nineveh was a very important city - a visit required three days. (Jonah 3:1-3)

This gracious second chance allows Jonah to get back on track in spite of first avoiding his responsibility by going on the shadow journey. Subsequently, he begins and successfully finishes phase three, his preaching mission (Jonah 3:4-10).

Unfortunately, Jonah's sinfulness is once again manifested during his phase four reflections. Rather than rejoicing in Nineveh's repentance, Jonah angrily reveals his prejudice and hatred toward the Assyrians. He cannot find the grace to celebrate God's compassionate and loving outreach to one of Israel's most feared enemies (Jonah 4:1-3, 11).

Phase four involves not only reaching a goal but also learning lessons from the journey experience. God forces Jonah to confront and reflect on the inappropriateness of his anger and on his selfishness. Thus, Jonah's spiritual journey is not truly complete until he discovers that God's concern for Israel's enemies is a legitimate and morally necessary expression of a Creator's love for humanity (Jonah 4:4-11).

The Apostles are Unwilling to Let
Their Journeys Conclude

As Jesus prepared for his sacrificial death on the cross, Peter, Judas and the other disciples were also facing the ending of a journey - their educational journey as Jesus' special disciples. Instead of embracing and celebrating this phase four time, as Jesus attempts to do during the Last Supper, the disciples give in to temptation and deny the essence of phase four by refusing to follow Jesus to Calvary. Each in his own way denies his Lord just as the journey is about to reach its climax. *This denial, manifested in a variety of ways, symbolizes the entry of sin into their phase four experience.*

For the disciples as a group, this denial takes the form of not being willing to recognize and acknowledge that Jesus is going to die. Jesus says to them, "Now I am going to him who sent me, yet none of you asks me, 'Where are you going?' . . . I have much more to say to you, more than you can now bear" (John 16:5, 12). In response, all they can say is "We don't understand what he is saying" (John 16:18). Earlier, they had manifested this same inability to comprehend Jesus' rather clear predictions:

> "Do not let your hearts be troubled. Trust in God; trust also in me. In my Father's house are many rooms; if it were not so, I would have told you. I am going there to prepare a place for you. And if I go and prepare a place for you, I will come back and take you to be with me that you also may be where I am. You know the way to the place where I am going." Thomas said to him, "Lord, we don't know where you are going, so how can we know the way?" (John 14:1-5)

This unwillingness to deal with Jesus' message ultimately leads to the disciples' abandonment of Jesus as He faithfully embraces His phase four death experience on the Cross. Jesus himself predicts this breaking of the link between Him and His supposedly faithful disciples. The following is His response to one of their faith confessions (John 16:30): "You believe at last! But a time is coming, and has come, when you will be scattered, each to his own home. You will leave me all alone. Yet I am not alone, for my Father is with me" (John 16:31-32).

Peter's threefold denial of Jesus (Matthew 26:69-75; Mark 14:66-72; Luke 22:54-62; John 18:15-27) is predicted specifically by Jesus as well:

> "Simon, Simon, Satan has asked to sift you as wheat. But I have prayed for you, Simon, that your faith may not fail. And when you have turned back, strengthen your brothers." But he replied, "Lord, I am ready to go with you to prison and to death." Jesus answered, "I tell you, Peter, before the rooster crows today, you will deny three times that you know me." (Luke 22:31-34)

Whether born out of terror or anger, from watching Jesus reject his help at Gethsemane, from fear of being arrested and sentenced to death, or from some other deep psychological reason, Peter's denial separates him from Jesus and serves as a pathetic protest that their journeys are not linked. Yet, despite the denials, Peter's and Jesus' journeys have been linked. His unwillingness to be identified with Jesus at this crucial point is not a personal rejection of Jesus Himself. It is more likely a sign that Peter loses his courage to face the essence of phase four - death - just as Jesus finds a resurgence of resolve to embrace it and complete His journey. While Jesus almost triumphantly cries "the hour is near, and the Son of Man is betrayed into the hands of sinners. Rise, let us go!" (Matthew 26:45-46), Peter attempts to prevent the arrest through violent means and inhibits Jesus' journey to the cross.

Peter's denial period begins even before the street incidents following Jesus' arrest, and is premised on the indefensible notion that Peter knows better than Jesus how to deal with the demands of the journey. His denial, therefore, might stem from a loss of trust in Jesus' leadership, or from an impetuous presumption fueled by pride. In either case, Peter's denial might be traced back to a combination of character flaw, ignorance and circumstance. The result of Peter's denial is his (temporary) separation from Jesus, an inability to participate actively in Jesus' phase four experience, and an inner sense of despair and bitterness. Instead of weeping for Jesus, or for sinners in need of God's love, Peter is reduced to weeping for himself.

Judas' denial of Jesus, at first glance, bears a remarkable similarity to Peter's. Both betray and deny Jesus during phase four of His spiritual journey, leave Him to his fate, and are deeply remorseful after

91

their unfaithful actions. Why, then, is Judas the villain and Peter the restored disciple?

We may put aside the judgment that Satan inspired Judas (Luke 22:3; John 13:2, 27), since Jesus also states that Satan was after Peter as well. Perhaps the answer lies in the motives behind Judas' denial of Jesus and the ending of his spiritual journey with the other disciples. Both Matthew and Mark associate Jesus' Bethany anointing by an unnamed woman with Judas' betrayal, but acknowledge that other disciples besides Judas had trouble with the act (Matthew 26:6-16; Mark 14:1-11). John explicitly identifies her as Mary of Bethany and records Judas' angry criticism of her action based on the needs of the poor (John 12:1-11). Yet even John admits that Judas was not really concerned about the poor: "He did not say this because he cared about the poor but because he was a thief; as keeper of the moneybag, he used to help himself to what was put into it" (John 12:6).

One possible motive for Judas' denial is his sense that his source of income is about to be cut off. If this is the case, then he is alone among the disciples in understanding that Jesus' explanation of the anointing involved a prediction of his imminent death: "Leave her alone. It was intended that she should save this perfume for the day of my burial. You will always have the poor among you, but you will not always have me" (John 12:7-8).

The Japanese Roman Catholic novelist Shusaku Endo peers into Judas' heart at this point in the story and, employing the imagination of a master fiction writer, uncovers an even deeper motive for Judas' betrayal of Jesus:

> Judas recognized as well as anyone else why Mary did what she had done. The author of John's Gospel interprets the outburst of Judas as a piece of hypocrisy. But the words of Judas imply something deeper. Judas is saying it clearly - that Jesus will never become the messiah that everyone seeks. While the rest of the disciples were no better than the pilgrims in their ignorance of the mind of Jesus, within the group Judas Iscariot alone was aware of the master's secret. Judas however, knowing what he knew, was far from happy with what he knew. . . Judas alone was capable of getting the point of the master's reply. He alone sensed how there was to be no switch in the master's destiny.

92

What is more, Judas even imagined to himself how his fellow disciples would all abandon Jesus when the time would come. For the moment, however, Judas was the only one to conceive that Jesus might be arrested, might be tortured, might die, alone.[1]

Peter's phase four experience with Jesus may have been disrupted because of a combination of character flaw, ignorance and circumstance, but the same cannot be said of Judas. He refuses to embrace phase four of his journey with Jesus because of his insight and knowledge, and because he feels betrayed by Jesus' unwillingness to become the militaristic Messiah of popular Jewish imagination. Judas cuts off his participation in Jesus' journey prematurely because he rejects its goal, and in so doing, he rejects Jesus as well. From a heart steeped in anger and spite, Judas rejects the plan of God for Jesus and defiantly disassociates himself from it, even to the point of working against Jesus. His original journey is over, and has been superseded by a sinful, shadow journey where cooperation with God has been replaced with cooperation with Jesus' adversaries. The perverse result, once the betrayal is accomplished, is an inappropriate death experience for Judas; he takes his own life (Matthew 27:1-10).

In stark contrast, Peter's phase four betrayal, grounded in fear rather than willful defiance, is forgiven by Jesus in a heart-wrenching scene recorded in John's gospel alone:

> When they had finished eating, Jesus said to Simon Peter, "Simon son of John, do you truly love me more than these?" "Yes, Lord," he said, "you know that I love you."
>
> Jesus said, "Feed my lambs." Again Jesus said, "Simon son of John, do you truly love me?" He answered, "Yes, Lord, you know that I love you." Jesus said, "Take care of my sheep." The third time he said to him, "Simon son of John, do you love me?"
>
> Peter was hurt because Jesus asked him the third time, "Do you love me?" He said, "Lord, you know all things; you know that I love you." Jesus said, "Feed my sheep. I tell you the truth, when you were younger you dressed yourself and went where you wanted; but when you are old you will stretch out your hands, and someone else will dress you and lead you where you do not want to go." Jesus said this to indicate the kind of death by

which Peter would glorify God. Then he said to him, "Follow me!" (John 21:15-19)

Jesus, now Himself in phase five of His journey, seeks to complete Peter's phase four experience by offering him reconciliation, symbolized by the question "do you truly love me more than these?", and the hope of a new journey call based on the concept of *agape* - the kind of sacrificial love that was expressed in Jesus' phase four death experience. Peter is going to be called to "feed" Jesus' followers and, as part of the fulfillment of his journey, experience a death that will glorify God. For Peter, a new journey is about to begin, and he will not make the same phase four mistake again.

Satan Opposes the Spiritual Journeys of God's People

The apocalyptic vision of Revelation 12-14 focuses on the spiritual warfare being waged between the forces of evil and God's people (Revelation 12:17; 13:7). Stated simply, the theme of this vision is that *Satan always opposes the spiritual journeys of God's people.* His goal is to "lead the whole world astray" (Revelation 12:9), meaning that he seeks to have humanity forsake our allegiance to God, the goals or destinations of our God-ordained journeys, and our freedom (Revelation 13:16-17). Instead of following Christ, he tries to convince us to "follow the beast" and "worship" him (Revelation 13:3-4), and to embrace shadow journeys which do not honor God.

In pursuit of his goal of dominating the world, Satan will stop at nothing, because "he knows his time is short" (Revelation 12:12). He realizes that the only way to succeed is to prevent the spiritual journeys of God's people from reaching their God-ordained conclusions. The devil's strategies of derailing spiritual journeys can be analyzed according to the phases of the Goal-Oriented Spiritual Journey Paradigm.

In phase one, *Satan tries to prevent our spiritual journeys from even beginning.* The vision states that he "stood in front of the woman who was about to give birth, so that he might devour her child the moment it was born" (Revelation 12:4). Within history, this refers to

94

Herod's attempt to kill Jesus (Matthew 2:16-18). In the Old Testament, this same strategy is employed by Pharaoh during the power encounter with Moses, when he rescinds permission for the slaves to leave Egypt (Exodus 8:15, 32; 9:34-35; 10:20).

In phase two, *Satan attempts to convince us not to embrace our journeys*. In the vision, this is symbolized by the contrast between the people whose names were never in the book of life (Revelation 13:8-10) and those who are redeemed (Revelation 14:1-5). The former embark on a shadow journey as slaves to evil (Revelation 13:15-18), while the latter group journeys in purity towards God. Jonah's initial refusal to journey to Nineveh illustrates the same point.

In phase three, *Satan attempts to bring to a halt or sidetrack a journey that is already progressing*. He has several strategies at his disposal in this regard.

In the Revelation 12 vision, Satan tries to "overtake the woman and sweep her away with the torrent" of flowing water which spewed forth from his mouth (Revelation 12:15). Pharaoh attempts to catch up to Moses and the Jews before they cross the Red Sea (Exodus 14). Satan tempts Jesus in an attempt to sidetrack his messianic journey right at the start of phase three (Matthew 4:1-11; Luke 4:1-13). In our journeys, Satan tries to rush upon us and disorient us so that we will not journey in the right direction.

Later in the Revelation vision, Satan tries to "astonish" (Revelation 13:3) people so that they will willingly leave the journey proposed by God. This "razzle-dazzle" approach often employs miracles and false signs to confuse the spiritually naive (Revelation 13:3, 12-13). This is a form of spiritual "deception" (Revelation 13:14), a well-tested strategy that Satan has used since the time of Adam and Eve (Genesis 3:1-13).

Fear and intimidation are also used by Satan as he "makes war" against God's people (Revelation 12:17). If he can awe us with his power, we will become too afraid to journey forward (Revelation 13:4). We see this in the Exodus story when Joshua and Caleb try to convince Israel to enter the promised land (Numbers 13-14). In the vision, intimidation is employed by the beast to "force" everyone to obey his rules (Revelation 13:16). Satan is also not adverse to sending "messengers" to "torment" us in order to halt the journey (2 Corinthians 12:7).

These considerations explain why Elijah can be so fearless at Mt. Carmel (1 Kings 18:20-46), and then flee timidly after Jezebel's death threat (1 Kings 19:1-8). In most spiritual journeys, phase three involves the overcoming of a number of challenges that eventually lead to the achievement of the journey's goal. In order to reach the goal (phase four), we must pace ourselves, use our spiritual energy and resources wisely, and remember that there is often a mental/emotional let-down following the fulfilling of a phase three challenge; none of us can remain on a spiritual high for an extended period of time. Elijah's Mt. Carmel experience was powerful, and it was inevitable that he would experience a corresponding let-down when it was over. Jezebel's death threat reaches Elijah during this vulnerable time. Elijah's feelings of isolation and loneliness (1 Kings 19:10) often accompany phase three let-downs or depressions.

God's response to Elijah's depression is to strengthen him by providing both food and spiritual encouragement (1 Kings 19:4-18). As we face our own phase 3 challenges, we can count on God to provide us with the spiritual resources we need to overcome them, and we can also count on God to sustain us during the inevitable let-downs that we will experience as the journey progresses.

Satan doesn't give up attempting to derail a journey even when it is about to come to a conclusion (phase four). The climax of Israel's spiritual journey was to give birth to the Messiah - this was the whole point of the journey. John's vision in Revelation shows Satan at the end of this journey doing everything possible to deny God's will (Revelation 12:1-4). Luke 22 records two attempts to influence Judas and Peter to oppose Jesus' journey just as phase four commences.

The Revelation 12 vision twice states what the response of God's people should be to Satan's attempts to derail our journeys:

> "This calls for *patient endurance and faithfulness* on the part of the saints." (Revelation 13:10)

> "This calls for *patient endurance* on the part of the saints who obey God's commandments and *remain faithful to Jesus.*" (Revelation 14:12)

If we patiently endure to the end of our journeys, remain faithful to the Lord of the journey and "resist" Satan's attacks (1 Peter 5:9), we will enjoy the rewards of phase five of the journey - God's rest and blessing (Revelation 14:13).

Chapter Six

All of Life Is a Journey

Spiritual Journeying and Our Lives

The Goal-Oriented Spiritual Journey Paradigm is not only a helpful tool in understanding the progress of Old and New Testament pilgrims, but is also applicable to the spiritual journeys of contemporary disciples of Jesus Christ. Discovering God's call and fulfilling it are as essential to our spiritual lives today as it was for Jesus, Peter, Paul and their followers.

Most Christians have a great deal of difficulty articulating God's will for their lives and how His presence intersects with their actual experiences. Doctrine does not help here, for the problem is not intellectual but experiential. People need descriptive language that is accessible to even new believers and yet profound enough to do justice to the spiritual journey experiences of the most mature disciples. We must adopt a world-view that is both consistent with Biblical teachings and human experience.

This is the objective of the Goal-Oriented Spiritual Journey Paradigm. It provides a comprehensive framework from which to discern, validate and articulate the progress of our spiritual journeys without dictating any specific content limitations on those journeys. It describes the flow of one's spiritual journey but does not prescribe its unique goals, modes of revelation, or pathways of activity. Only God can provide us with a specific goal to fulfill, and He alone decides how this goal is to be revealed to us. The paradigm reminds us that it's time to cooperate with God and others, and calls us to exercise responsibility in fulfilling the journey. When a journey reaches its conclusion, the paradigm assists us in learning journey lessons. During phase five, the paradigm assures us that a new journey is just around the corner.

The Goal-Oriented Spiritual Journey Paradigm, above all, calls us to appreciate the journeys of our life and to embrace them with faith and faithfulness.

Faith and Faithfulness

Faith (Gk. *pistis*) is the foundation of our spiritual journeys. Faith has nothing to do with emotions or selfish desires to get things from God, but consists of "being sure of what we hope for and certain of what we do not see" (Hebrews 11:1). This refers to our certainty concerning our heavenly destination, the ultimate goal of our earthly journeys. Hebrews affirms the spiritual journeys of Abraham, Isaac and Jacob (Hebrews 11:8-21) because they "were longing for a better country - a heavenly one" (Hebrews 11:16).

This hope in God's promise of "a kingdom that cannot be shaken" (Hebrews 12:28) enables us to endure challenges throughout our journeys and to "run with perseverance the race marked out for us" (Hebrews 12:1). Thus, "without faith it is impossible to please God, because anyone who comes to him must believe that he exists and that he rewards those who earnestly seek him" (Hebrews 11:6).

In contrast to the Jewish prophets and heros of the faith (Hebrews 11:4-38), the Jews of the Exodus did not respond to God by faith and thus were unable to complete their spiritual journey (Hebrews 3-4). They neither believed in Yahweh (they clung to their idols, according to the prophets) or embraced in their hearts the goal of the journey, and thus their phase three experience was marked not by cooperation (with God and Moses) but rather by unbelief, disobedience and sin (Hebrews 3:7-4:11). There can be no faithfulness when faith is absent.

Did you ever wonder why the prostitute Rahab is listed in the honor roll of faithful people in Hebrews 11:31? In light of her occupation, her story is an ironic portrayal of the role that *faithfulness* should play in our relationships and journeys. After "dealing kindly" (Hebrew, *hesed*) by protecting two Jewish spies, she asks them to swear in return that they will show "kindness" (*hesed*) by pledging "honestly" (Hebrew, *emeth* - truth) to spare her family during the upcoming invasion (Joshua 2:12-13). The spies agree (Joshua 2:14) to treat her with "kindness and truth" (*hesed* and *emeth*).

Hesed is a magnificent Hebrew word which is usually translated as *faithfulness*. It signifies our obligation to others, whether they be relatives, friends, God, or sometimes even strangers. It denotes loyalty, solidarity, faithfulness in keeping our covenants, or in returning favors, kindness, and grace. In Exodus 34:6, *hesed* characterizes God's relationship with His people. Whenever our journeys are linked to the journeys of others, *hesed* should define the covenantal nature of the relationship.

Emeth is another beautiful Hebrew word which signifies reliability, lasting kindness, fidelity, and truthfulness in our relationships. Abraham's slave, after meeting Rebekah, praises God by saying that God "has not forsaken His lovingkindness (*hesed*) and His truth (*emeth*) towards my master" (Genesis 24:27). Rahab is a role model of faithfulness because she practices and asks for both *hesed* and *emeth* when the Jewish spies place their journeys into her hands. We might say that these two words epitomize all that God desires us to experience in our relationships with Him and other people. Covenant faithfulness is the essence of the relational side of Christianity, and no journey is worth living without it.

Faithfulness in fulfilling God's journey call is the major theme of Joshua's life. He is called to exercise faith by believing in God's power, having the courage to do God's will, being obedient to God's Word, and being positive in the face of tremendous challenges in light of God's promise to stand by him (Joshua 1:5-9). All of this is involved in fulfilling God's call to possess the land of Canaan. Similarly, as we seek to express faith and faithfulness throughout our spiritual journeys, we must continually reflect on the course of our journeys, recognize recurring journey themes, pray for guidance as our journeys progress, relate to others, grow in holiness, and hope for the eternal journey to come. We now turn our attention to these issues.

Reflecting on the Phases of Our Journeys

"What is God calling me to do?" Accomplished journeyers intuitively act in accordance with the rhythm described by the Goal-Oriented Spiritual Journey Paradigm even if they are unaware of the conceptual framework itself. For them, such an outline may seem artificial and unnecessary. On the other hand, it may give them a fresh appreciation of how God works in their lives, and it may serve to confirm their intuition.

For the majority of people who have trouble sensing how God is guiding their lives, a grasp of the five phases of the spiritual journey can give them a handle upon which to develop insight, new understanding, and an inner assurance that God truly is at work in their journeys. The key is to analyze our own journeys in the same way we reflected upon the Biblical journeys in this book. This involves the following steps:

• Identify the theme of the journey based on the phase two call. Begin your analysis of each journey at phase two so that you can next look back at phase one and forward to the later phases.

• Explore the dynamics of phase two by looking at the mode God chose to reveal His will, your reactions to the call experience, and the goal and target people which define the journey. Decide whether the phase two call summoned you to a redemptive or mission level journey.

• Look back through your past to see how God prepared you for the journey (phase one). Look at the ebb and flow of key relationships. Creatively examine past events to see how they have prepared you for the journey. It's amazing how isolated past experiences take on a whole new significance when examined in this light!

• Chart the progress of phase three. Look for recurring patterns and milestones (successes and failures) along the way. Identify those experiences which highlight the ways you cooperated with God and others in order to achieve the journey goal.

• If you are examining a journey which has already concluded, re-assess the significance of the journey. Remember, phase four is characterized by reflection, worship and often a sense of grieving. What wisdom did you gain because you experienced this journey? Since faithfulness is the key determinant of whether God sees the journey as a success or failure, assess honestly how faithful you were in each of the phases.

• Since phase five connects one journey to the next, examining this final phase provides you with an excellent opportunity to appreciate how a specific journey is linked to the others you have experienced.

• Remember that God does not call you to travel as an isolated individual, but as a member of a spiritual community. Your journeys are often linked to the journeys of other people and to the corporate journey of your local church. Reflect on these links and appreciate their importance and sacredness.

You do not have to wait until the conclusion of a journey to begin examining it. The Goal-Oriented Spiritual Journey Paradigm can help you identify the present phase of a journey. Armed with such knowledge, you can then act in a phase appropriate manner and ask phase appropriate questions in order to further the journey in the most efficient manner.

Recognizing Recurring Themes
Which Impact Our Journeys

In each of our lives, certain general themes manifest themselves repeatedly across spiritual journeys. These themes are not journeys in and of themselves, but they influence the course and outcome of our several journeys.

In Jacob's life, the recurring themes are "taking what is not yours" and "deception." Early in his life (at his birth, and when he steals Esau's birthright and blessing), he does both of these things. However, in his "wife-seeking" journey (Genesis 29-31), he becomes the victim of these themes - he has met his match in Laban!

It is to our advantage to recognize the recurring themes in our lives, and to learn from them. Jacob comes to this realization just in the nick of time, and this enables him to prepare properly and wisely for his reunion with Esau (Genesis 32-33). By facing his recurring journey themes, he is able to reconcile with a former foe, which in turn enables him to finish his journey.

Recurring themes also manifest themselves in a group's historical experience. The book of Judges records many of Israel's journeys (each one represented by a judge) during the period between Joshua's conquest and the beginning of the monarchy. Despite the differing specific circumstances of each journey, all share a common recurring theme: Israel's unfaithfulness to God which leads to judgment (Judges 2:10-22). In this case, the reader comes to the sad realization that Israel never learned from its recurring theme, despite repeated attempts by the prophets to educate them. And, as a result, journey after journey ends in failure or disaster.

Since recurring themes can have such a dramatic impact on our journeys, it is essential that we discover them during the course of our reflections. Some themes are positive and constructively advance our journeys, while others represent negative and destructive tendencies which hinder our progress.

In our lives, both kinds of themes exist and must be acknowledged. The positive themes are symbols of God's grace and should be appreciated. The negative themes must be listened to and faced honestly so that their impact can be minimized or reversed.

Praying in Light of Our Journeys

Our personal and corporate spiritual journeys are the context for our prayer life and our relationship with God. Unless we fall into the trap of viewing our experiences with God as unconnected self-contained events, it is clear that God always relates to us in and through the spiritual journeys we embrace (or reject, as in Jonah's case). *Prayer, then, should be understood as a spiritual journey-based exercise.* Its purpose is to help us experience and maintain a proper orientation to God so that we may faithfully fulfill our journeys in accordance with God's will.

This spiritual journey-based understanding of prayer helps us avoid another trap which has ensnared so many contemporary Christians - the notion that prayer is the means by which we get our desires and needs met by God. This common conception of prayer encourages self- centeredness by visualizing the Lord of the universe as a glorified errand boy who has nothing better to do than fuss over our whims, dreams, and comfort. It also assumes that a strong prayer life can be measured by the affirmative answers we receive.

While it is true that God answers our prayers and often provides us with many things we ask for (Matthew 7:7-12; Luke 11:1-13; Philippians 4:6), we must admit that just as often He apparently chooses to deny our requests (James 4:1-3). Two people, both with faith, have a disease and pray for healing; one receives it, while the other does not. Two people pray for the same job; only one can fill the position. Two people fall in love with the same person; only one gets the privilege of experiencing a relationship.

If we are honest, we must conclude that God does not answer prayers based on what we want or desire, but rather on a complex set of considerations which we signify by the phrase "God's will" (see Matthew 6:10). Thus, John affirms: "This is the confidence we have in approaching God: that if we ask anything *according to his will*, he hears us" (1 John 5:14).

Since God's will is that we journey toward the goals He has ordained for us, our prayer life should focus not on our perceived needs as ends in themselves, but rather *on God's self- revelation and our needs in light of the circumstances and demands of our journeys.*

This is Jesus' very point in the Sermon on the Mount when he admonishes us to stop worrying about material and personal needs. They are not ends in themselves even though we place such importance on them. God is aware of our needs, and supplies the necessities of life without being asked. Worry, reflecting an undue preoccupation with our own needs, is a sign of lack of faith (Matthew 6:25-32). Instead, we should place our needs in context by focusing on our role in representing the kingdom of God: "But seek first his kingdom and his righteousness, and all these things will be given to you as well" (Matthew 6:33). We fulfill our kingdom responsibilities by embracing and living out our spiritual journeys.

God will provide us with whatever is needed to further our journeys. He appropriately denies requests which will not positively impact our journeys, as in the case of the favor asked for by the Zebedee sons' mother (Matthew 20:20-28). When we presumptuously persist in requesting selfish indulgences which will not further our journeys, God may punish us by giving in to us. The classic example is the Exodus story of the Israelites demanding quail (Numbers 11:4-34). Prayer, therefore, increases our awareness of who the Lord of our journey is and what is required to complete the journey. Prayer helps us discipline ourselves even to the point of personal denial in order to fulfill the journey call (1 Corinthians 9:24-27).

Praying in light of our journeys requires *honesty* on our part as we relate to God and assess the themes and progress of each journey. The Samaritan woman at the well was not permitted to begin her spiritual journey until after she had stopped lying to Jesus about her past and present relationships (John 4:4-26, 39-42). Embracing honesty is the first step in seeking wisdom, which we may define as the insight necessary to fulfill a spiritual journey. Our awareness of our lack of wisdom leads us to pray for it, and God assures us that this is one prayer He wants to answer (James 1:5)!

Spiritual journey-based prayer seeks wisdom by focusing on the specific needs and questions arising out of each spiritual journey phase. Nehemiah reminds us that a successful spiritual life is dependent on the seriousness with which we integrate God into our journeys (Nehemiah 1:11, 2:20). God is not a distant deity that must be ritually satisfied, but rather a personal Lord who guides and protects us as we journey (Nehemiah 2:12, 4:9, 7:5). Each phase of the journey is an opportunity to seek God's presence, ask penetrating questions, and listen for wisdom and new marching orders.

During phase one, our prayers should focus on quieting our souls, patience and trust. It is not easy to wait for an authentic journey call, and our impatience causes us to want to rush the journey process so that "we can get on with it." We must avoid the temptation of chasing after journey possibilities that are actually mirages and dead-ends. It is difficult to feel secure during a phase that presents no discernable purpose, and hope, therefore, should be a central theme as we praise God. Phase one is an excellent opportunity to practice our listening skills in preparation for receiving God's call in phase two.

During phase two, our prayers should focus on discovering and embracing journey goals. The inner quietness we cultivated in phase one manifests itself in phase two as a receptive spirit. In this phase, the first task of prayer is to receive God's self-revelation and the unveiling of His will. Patience gives way to eagerness to embrace journey goals. Trust blossoms into submissiveness to God's will, and prayer reaches its pinnacle as we commit ourselves to the journey goals. We will be tempted during phase two to reject God's will and to shrink from embracing journey goals. We must resist distractions which pull us away from committing ourselves to the journey. We must be open to confessing our sins, so that we may begin the journey in a state of holiness.

During phase three, our prayers should focus on enhancing our cooperation with God and others. The receptive spirit of phase two now opens itself to the presence of the Holy Spirit during phase three. We should continually pray for the Spirit's guidance and anointing. Eagerness, which is sufficient to start the journey, grows into faithfulness; endurance and cooperation are virtues in this phase. Our prior willingness to submit to God's will now enables us to submit to others whose journeys have been linked to ours. We will be tempted to allow the journey to be sidetracked, and thus our prayers should help us focus on the priorities of reaching the journey goal and maintaining unity and a cooperative spirit among God's people.

During phase four, our prayers should focus on lessons learned and praise for the Lord of the journey. We celebrate God's power, present our faithfulness and perseverance as gifts to Him, and gain wisdom as we examine His will from the vantage point of the spiritual journey's conclusion.

During phase five, we rejoice in the power of Jesus' resurrection and begin to set our sights on the challenges of the future. Bolstered by new wisdom and deepened experience, we anticipate God's call to embrace new and exciting journeys.

Friends and Guides Along the Way

Proverbs stresses the importance of wisdom and key relationships (friends and guides) for those who embark on spiritual journeys. Proverbs 1-9 contains a series of poetic exhortations which encourage inexperienced journeyers to embrace God's wisdom and shun sinners in order to insure the success of the journey (Proverbs 8:32-36). The poet employs relational imagery to bring this message home. The father and mother of the son serve as spiritual directors (Proverbs 1:8; 4:10-11) for the young man who is about to leave home and strike out on his own.

He is reminded of all of the spiritual lessons (wisdom) his parents have given him through the years. They urge him to cherish and embrace "the wife of your youth" (Proverbs 5:18), lady wisdom (Proverbs 3:13-26), which means that he should allow wisdom to govern his heart and actions (Proverbs 2:1-2). By doing so, he will avoid the mistakes of others who have fallen into sin by following another woman. The harlot/adulterous woman represents evil, rebellion, unfaithfulness and her goal in enticing the journeyer is to destroy him (Proverbs 2:16-19; 5:3-20). Thus, as the young man begins his spiritual journey, he has a fundamental choice to make. His journey will lead him either toward spiritual life or death. If he embraces his spiritual parents and lady wisdom, he will find God (Proverbs 2:1-12). However, if he befriends sinners and the harlot, death will overtake him (Proverbs 1:10-19; 9:13-18).

Close relationships decisively impact our journeys. How could someone as wise as Solomon turn away from God towards the end of his journey? Solomon's love for his foreign princesses created within him a desire to satisfy their needs, and this allowed them to influence him to build "high places" designed for the worship of their idols (1 Kings 11:2-8). The Bible indicates that "the LORD was angry with Solomon because his heart was turned away from the LORD" (1 Kings 11:9) and blames his wives for this fall from complete devotion: "his wives turned his heart away after other gods" (1 Kings 11:4).

When we allow people to enter into our inner relational circles, they gain a measure of control over us that can be used either positively or negatively. We must be discriminating in our choice of close friends. If we wish to see our relationship with God flourish, we should chose intimate friends who are devoted to God and who will commit themselves to helping us fulfill our journeys.

Ruth's devotion to her mother-in-law, Naomi, is a beautiful example of the kind of love, commitment and loyalty which makes journeys flourish. After Naomi's husband and two sons die in Moab (Ruth 1:1-5), she decides to return to Israel. Initially, both Orpah and Ruth begin the journey with her, but Naomi urges them to reconsider because she could not give them new husbands. Orpah did return home, but Ruth "clung" to Naomi and remained devoted both to her mother-in-law and God (Ruth 1:7-21). Ruth's determination to stand by Naomi in the face of adversity is wonderful to see, especially since she had nothing to gain from this action (she could not have foreseen being redeemed by Boaz). Ruth's unselfishness is a hallmark of true friendship. She is no "fair weather" friend, but rather a woman who models a covenantal faithfulness which enhances everyone's journeys.

David's relationship with Jonathan, Saul's son, is another excellent example of the covenantal nature of true friendship. Both pledged loyalty and faithfulness (*hesed*) even when it was not in their own interest to do so (1 Samuel 18:3; 20:1-23; 23:18). The friendship caused Jonathan to defend and encourage David even when he was fighting against his own father (1 Samuel 20:30-34; 23:16-17). Their commitment to each other's journeys is a challenge to us all as we consider how we might support the journeys of our friends.

These two examples of same-sex friendships (Ruth and Naomi, David and Jonathan) indicate that our faith in God is lived out in and through the close relationships we establish with those around us. In an age where the sexual dimension of relationships is emphasized to an extreme, these stories remind us that commitment and caring are at the core of true friendship, and that true friendship furthers journeys.

Friends do not have to be on identical journeys in order to journey together. The journeys of Ezra and Nehemiah are complementary, but not identical. Ezra's goal, as the religious teacher and scribe (Ezra 7:6), is to ground the new settlers in the Jewish faith (Ezra 7:10; Nehemiah 8:1-8). Nehemiah's goal, as the nation's governor, is to protect Israel from outside enemies by rebuilding the walls of Jerusalem (Nehemiah 1:3, 2:5; 5:14). Neither man could achieve his aim without the other's cooperation and support, and thus their journeys were linked.

There are times in all of our lives when we need not just a friend, but a spiritual guide who can make up for the experience we may lack. Such people can give us perspective, wisdom, objective advice and discerning support as we seek God's will. They can also assist us in facing the key challenges of each journey phase. Samuel's phase two experience is mediated through a vision, but his spiritual inexperience necessitates the discernment of Eli, a spiritual director. Eli helps the young man discover God's call and also confirms the validity of the experience (1 Samuel 3:7-18).

Holiness as Both Means and End

Holiness serves as both a means and an end as we journey. When Paul declares that he wishes to "press on toward the goal to win the prize for which God has called me heavenward in Christ Jesus" (Philippians 3:14), he is looking forward to the time when his journey toward holiness will be completed. How eagerly he anticipates receiving "the crown of righteousness" which Jesus will grant him in the future (2 Timothy 4:8)!

Journeying towards holiness transports us from the earthly to the heavenly realm (Colossians 3:1-4). In this sense, it has always been the vision of Christian pilgrims to embrace holiness as the end or goal of the Christian life: "It is God's will that you should be sanctified . . . for God did not call us to be impure, but to live a holy life" (1 Thessalonians 4:3, 7). Throughout this life, therefore, we should engage in redemptive-level journeys in order to grow ever more Christ-like.

As a means, virtues gained through previous journeys provide a solid foundation for the mission-level journeys we embrace throughout life. The progressive attainment of holiness in our past is part of any journey's phase one preparation (as demonstrated so well by the Jerusalem church's deacon selection process in Acts 6:1-7). Every spiritual journey implicitly presupposes that some measure of godliness has already been attained in the life of the journeyer.

As we face the challenges of our spiritual journeys and develop perseverance, our godliness is tested in the crucible of human experience. When we see we are lacking in some area of personal integrity or maturity, we may call upon God to provide us with additional wisdom and virtue in order to facilitate the fulfillment of our tasks. Whatever we lack, God will provide (James 1:2-5).

Specific spiritual journeys (of both the redemptive and mission varieties) provide a context in which God may help us discover our growing edges in regard to godliness and then attain higher levels of holiness. Goal-oriented journeys, accordingly, significantly contribute to the success of the journey toward perfection (holiness as an end). The Goal-Oriented Spiritual Journey Paradigm, in its articulation of the relationship between holiness as a lifelong goal and mission-related tasks as that which should occupy our attention in the short-term, highlights the bond that exists between faith and works, between inner spiritual growth and outer-world service, between personal maturity and our responsibility to impact society in a positive manner:

If anyone considers himself religious and yet does not keep a tight rein on his tongue, he deceives himself and his religion is worthless. Religion that God our Father accepts as pure and faultless is this: to look after orphans and widows in their distress and to keep oneself from being polluted by the world. (James 1:26-27)

Eternal Life: Our Future Spiritual Journey

When Christian mystics approach the subject of our heavenly journey, words are replaced by poetry, metaphors or silence. How can one adequately describe eternity when one is caught in the clutches of mortality, or picture perfect love and perfection of spirit while still living in a world of unfaithfulness and imperfection?

Unlike the baffled Thomas, we do "know the way" and we, through faith, also have a sense of where we are going (John 14:5). However, the nature of our experiences throughout the forthcoming eternal existence still remains a mystery, an unknown. The Scriptures point toward heaven as our destination, but provide few details concerning its nature. We can at least affirm that heaven is the existence where we worship the Lord in purity of faith, love and holiness (Hebrews 12:22-24; Revelation 4:1-11). Even Jesus rarely discloses what heavenly life will be like. In fact, on one of the few occasions when he even addressed the issue, all he would say is that:

At the resurrection people will neither marry nor be given in marriage; they will be like the angels in heaven. But about the resurrection of the dead - have you not read what God said to you, 'I am the God of Abraham, the God of Isaac, and the God of Jacob'? He is not the God of the dead but of the living." (Matthew 22:30-32)

Why will there be no marriage in heaven? In this life, marriage signifies the deepest relationship possible, and is ideally reserved for a unique one-to-one coupling of complementary opposites (male and female). In heaven, however, the horizontal unitive experience is replaced by a vertical one; we will be married to God (Revelation 19:6-9; 21:2-4).

111

What then, of our relationship to one another? In heaven, every relationship will transcend the deepest relationship possible here on earth, because we will no longer need to maintain secrets or relational distance from one another. Our relationships will be deeper, more honest and more open than even the closest relationship we may enjoy on earth. Marriage to an individual becomes an obsolete notion in heaven because it loses its uniqueness. This is possible because the heavenly existence (the marriage between God and us) promises an intellectual and relational perfection, in addition to moral perfection. Love in heaven is coupled with perfect self-knowledge and a perfect knowledge of God (1 Corinthians 13:8-12).

Similarly, 1 John admits that "what we will be has not yet been made known. But we know that when he appears, we shall be like him, for we shall see him as he is. Everyone who has this hope in him purifies himself, just as he is pure" (1 John 3:2-3). Paul prophesies that in the future God's glory will be "revealed in us" when we are adopted and redeemed, and all of creation will be "liberated from its bondage to decay and brought into the glorious freedom of the children of God" (Romans 8:18-25). But then what?

This description of eternal life is frustrating to many, for in some ways it still avoids the core spiritual journey questions that all of us have asked at one time or another. What will we do when we get to heaven? How will we spend the days of eternity? Does eternity have a purpose (beyond worship)? What challenges or tasks await us? Is heaven an ending or a new beginning?

The Goal-Oriented Spiritual Journey Paradigm implicitly affirms that there must be significant journeys and tasks awaiting us in heaven, and throughout eternity. Goal-oriented journeying does not cease when we enter eternal life. The heavenly marriage metaphor demands the anticipation of new challenges in eternity. Phase two of our spiritual journey in heaven is described as a "wedding" between Christ and God's people (Revelation 19:7-9). Weddings celebrate not the ending of a journey but its beginning. Therefore, the wedding ceremony in heaven symbolizes that when our spiritual journeys are completely linked to Christ's, new goal-oriented journeys will commence.

The general recurring theme of these future goal-oriented journeys is revealed in the closing vision of Revelation:

No longer will there be any curse. The throne of God and of the Lamb will be in the city, and his servants will serve him. They will see his face, and his name will be on their foreheads. There will be no more night. They will not need the light of a lamp or the light of the sun, for the Lord God will give them light. And they will reign for ever and ever. (Revelation 22:3-5)

In eternity, we will continue to serve the Lord, and "reign" forever. Like Jesus, the servant-king, we will manifest the will of God by simultaneously acting as servants and people with authority. But whom will we serve? Over whom will we exercise authority? Unfortunately, no target group is ever revealed. The terms of the upcoming call will not be made fully known until this earthly journey is complete. Phase two of a new journey - one's call - is not given by God until prior journeys have been fulfilled.

If phase two of our eternal goal-oriented journey will not begin until we complete all of our earthly journeys, then it is possible to view all of this life as a general phase one experience, a preparation for what is awaiting us in eternity. Every day of our lives, and every journey we embrace, has a significance beyond what we can know. We are being prepared for eternal journeys which remain unannounced to us because they are hidden in the heart of God. This is characteristic of phase one.

Nevertheless, we can be certain that what we do in this life impacts the role we will play in the kingdom of God in eternity. Jesus says, "For the Son of Man is going to come in his Father's glory with his angels, and then he will reward each person according to what he has done" (Matthew 16:27). In the parable of the faithful and unfaithful servants (Luke 12:35-48), the reward Jesus promises is linked to the twin ideas already referred; we will have further opportunities to serve, and the roles we will play will be greater if we are faithful in the journeys presently assigned. Some of us may even "be put in charge of all of his possessions" (Luke 12:44)!

Chapter Seven

Comparing Spiritual Journey Models

Appreciating Different Interpretations of Spiritual Journeys

The Goal-Oriented Spiritual Journey Paradigm is not the only model which can be used to interpret spiritual journey experience. Eastern religions in particular emphasize such exercises to a greater extent than doctrine. In this chapter, however, we will limit ourselves to surveying the two major paradigms which have had the greatest impact on Christianity, and compare them to the Goal-Oriented Spiritual Journey Paradigm.

Viewing the same journey from different perspectives changes our understanding of its course, dynamics and purpose. If we wish to see our journey experiences in a new way (which is the desire of many people today), then we must appreciate the old lights and their wisdom. Embracing new paradigms does not imply that older paradigms carry no value or insight. Instead, the challenge of a new paradigm is to assimilate the wisdom of previous models (while also adding new insights) so that this wisdom can appear in a fresh and more comprehensive guise and speak to a new audience.

We can generalize about the development of journey paradigms in Western history by affirming that there have been two broad answers to the question of the meaning of humanity's experience within the confines of Christianity - the *Classical Spiritual Journey Paradigm* and the *Modern Psychological Paradigm of Human Development.*

The Classical Spiritual Journey

The *Classical Spiritual Journey Paradigm* was articulated originally by the church fathers and flowered within the monastic movements of Roman Catholic and Orthodox Christianity from the fourth through sixteenth centuries. Protestantism, though negatively critiquing Catholic doctrine and church polity, nevertheless retained the broad outlines of the classical understanding of spiritual journey experience while modifying it to embody the more democratic ideals of the movement. Language and theology changed, but not the embracing of the underlying experience of Christ's mercy and grace, with the exceptions that such journey experience belonged not to the elite monks, but to all Christians, and that it was in all ways, the product of grace and faith as opposed to good works (an affirmation that few medieval mystics would deny).

The Classical Spiritual Journey Paradigm portrays Christian experience of the presence of God as a spiritual ascent of the soul towards God which progresses according to three distinct and consecutive stages: *purgation, illumination and union with God in love*. Protestants label the stages as *salvation, sanctification, and eternal life*. The focus and goal of the Christian journey is defined as holiness. The journey toward holiness culminates in moral, ethical and spiritual perfection.

The first stage, which the monks called *purgation*, represents the cleansing of the soul from all of its attachments to this world and its sinfulness. If the soul is to ascend toward heaven, it must be light enough to get off the ground. The confession and renunciation of sins provides the means of spiritual detachment from an ungodly culture. In medieval society, this step was symbolized by a vivid act of faith - the withdrawal from the world into the realm of the monastery. Later, in the more Anabaptist and pietistic forms of Protestantism, adult or believer's baptism served symbolically in the same capacity.

The second stage, *illumination*, represents the gradual progress the soul makes in drawing closer to God through the acquisition of virtues and the continuing battle against vices. During this stage the soul falls deeper and deeper in love with God as the latter alternatively manifests His presence and absence. Illumination depends on the power of the Holy Spirit to change and guide the soul through the manifold temptations, trials and challenges of life. Along the path, wisdom is gained and wedded to knowledge.

Since in this stage the soul matures spiritually by appropriating the fruit of the Spirit, Protestants prefer to label this stage as *sanctification*. Such growth is described in many creative ways by the mystics. St. John Climacus likens this journey to climbing up the steps

116

of a ladder. St. John of the Cross envisions it as the soul's search for its absent lover (Christ). Theresa of Avila portrays it as the moving from one room to another in a great castle. The greatest Protestant description of this stage (and indeed, the entire three stage journey) is The Pilgrim's Progress by John Bunyan. Christian's journey through hills and valleys towards the Celestial City is a profound portrait of the challenges implicit in journeying according to the Classical Paradigm. Since the journey can be so dangerous, gaining advice and counsel from wise spiritual guides (monks, pastors, bishops, etc.) often determines whether the journey proceeds in a positive manner. Spiritual direction provides the wisdom for the journey.

The third stage of the Classical Spiritual Journey Paradigm, *union with God in love*, follows death and represents reaching the destination of the soul's journey toward God. In heaven, the soul is perfectly united forever with God and experiences love in the fullest possible way. With sin no longer able to create any kind of separation between God and the soul, the soul is able to receive and express love with God in complete holiness and perfection. This is the wonder and essence of eternal life. Although reserved for the future, the joy of this stage is graciously mediated to the soul at various points throughout the illuminative stage by means of mystical or "peak" (as Abraham Maslow calls them) religious experiences. These high points of spiritual growth and experience, though often intense, are short-lived and, in this life, cannot be sustained by the soul. They do serve as powerful encouragement to continue the journey to its conclusion.

The Journey of Human Development

In the late nineteenth century, a profound and revolutionary paradigm emerged from the secular world of science. Beginning with Freud and continuing today through various schools of developmental psychology, an individual's journey may be described in radically different terms than those offered by the Classical Paradigm. The psychologically-based stage theories advanced by Freud, Jung, Piaget, Erikson and Kohlberg have gained wide acceptance and thus symbolize the extent to which a revolutionary paradigm shift has occurred.

The Modern Psychological Paradigm is decidedly *anthropo*centric. The journey is analyzed not from the perspective of spirituality, but from psychology, in effect cutting off the necessity of divine intervention or interaction with the process. The journeys described by secular psychological models are not faith-specific, but rather are held to be operative in people's lives as a natural phenomenon, irrespective of one's personal beliefs about God. It is no wonder that in this paradigm a significant shift of perspective takes place. The paradigm is not concerned with a *spiritual* ascent, but with a human centered *developmental* ascent towards reaching one's potential.

The shift from a theocentric to an anthropocentric developmental world view profoundly affects the Modern Psychological Paradigm's understanding of the goal of the journey. In place of the Classical Paradigm's goal of the spiritual journey as union with God in the afterlife, the Modern Psychological Paradigm envisions the goal of the journey as being reached potentially in this world and defines it in terms of human potential, wholeness, health and fulfillment.

The Modern Psychological Paradigm views the human journey in biological or physical terms, and thus begins the journey at birth. Throughout this life, development of human potential continues until life itself ceases. Thus, the horizons for the psychological paradigm are birth and death, the beginning and ending of our life in this world.

The Modern Psychological Paradigm replaces God's grace with the natural and impersonal process of human maturation, which as a force unto itself is not controllable by the person undergoing it (a child does not consciously decide to move from the oral to the anal stage of psycho-sexual development, for example). For adults, change is induced not through divine forgiveness and grace, but through therapy, education or the gaining of personal insight into the dynamics that have shaped one's past and present. Instead of a reconciliation with God, the Modern Psychological Paradigm asserts the necessity of a reconciliation with oneself and one's past.

The paradigm shift from the Classical to the Psychological model necessitates a corresponding shift in guides for the journey. In the later paradigm, the spiritual guide is replaced by the psychological counselor/therapist. Carl Gustav Jung writes:

> It is significant that the psychological doctor (within my experience) is consulted more by Jews and Protestants than by Catholics. This might be expected, for the Catholic Church still

feels responsible for the *cura animarum* (the care of the soul's welfare). But in this scientific age, the psychiatrist is apt to be asked the questions that once belonged to the domain of the theologian.[1]

Like the Classical Paradigm, the Modern Psychological Paradigm employs stage or phase language to describe the course of human journeys. The stages are often based on singular developmental themes (psychosexual, cognitive, social, etc.). Sigmund Freud's five stages of psychosexual development (*oral, anal, phallic, latency, and genital*), for example, are virtually household terms. Progress through these stages impacts one's health, healing, maturation, individuation and wholeness.

Carl Gustav Jung's analytical psychology balances Freud's emphasis on childhood stages by highlighting the significance of the psychospiritual dimensions of the adult portion of life. In The Stages of Life, Jung outlines three general stages of human psychological development: *childhood* (birth to puberty), *youth* (puberty to mid-life), and *the second half of life*. In this third stage of life we strive for *individuation*, which Jung defines as "the psychological process that makes of a human being an 'individual' - a unique, indivisible unit or 'whole man.'"[2]

Erik Erikson posits that the stages of a person's journey focus on how the individual relates to the outer world of one's family and society at large. He identifies eight stages from birth to old age that must be successfully dealt with in order for an individual to emerge as a healthy personality: trust versus mistrust (infancy), autonomy versus shame and doubt (early childhood), initiative versus guilt (play age), industry versus inferiority (early school years), identity versus identity diffusion (adolescence), intimacy versus isolation (young adult years), generativity versus self-absorption (middle adulthood), and integrity versus despair (mature age). Erikson defines this final period as the attaining and appreciating of wisdom.[3]

Integrating the Two Paradigms

There have been numerous attempts to integrate the two paradigms described in this chapter. Donald Capps advocates a

119

journey centered pastoral theology based on Erik Erikson's life cycle theory. His "therapeutic wisdom" model ministry envisions the pastor functioning as a moral counselor, ritual coordinator and personal comforter for people as they pass through the eight stage lifecycle. While it is clear that Capps' theology of a person's spiritual journey is based on the Modern Psychological Paradigm, he also seeks to acknowledge the Classical Paradigm's wisdom. Capps identifies "eight deadly vices" and eight corresponding "virtues" which must be grappled with as the psychosocial stages progress. Of course, the hope is that during each stage, the outcome of the struggle will be that the virtue breaks the vice's hold over us.[4]

Morton Kelsey's spiritual journey model, while based on Jung's and Erickson's insights, also incorporates such classical Christian devotional practices as dream interpretation, silence, solitude, and journaling. Kelsey sees "seven quite different stages of human development relevant to our *spiritual* growth."[5] The first stage involves the emergence of a child's personality so that he/she may later become capable of developing a loving relationship with God and of possessing faith. Childhood (stage 2) involves the development of an ego in order to discern the difference between the inner and outer worlds. During adolescence (stage 3) the child moves into the adult world, with all the spiritual struggles that this transition entails. Searching for meaning in life and attempting to relate to God on a young adult level (stage 4) may cause spiritual problems if an adequate form of spiritual care is unavailable. Stage 5 centers around the mid-life crisis. Stage 6 can be a "golden age" in which "we can reflect on and try to accomplish those things that will be most fulfilling to us and of greatest help to others." Stage 7 involves the challenge of facing the implications of our death.

Like Capps, Kelsey observes that spiritual direction can facilitate our passage through the developmental stages, which can be difficult to negotiate alone. Spiritual direction may also enable people to "live through a stage that they missed before," which is crucial because "the various stages each provide essential elements in a full and mature religious life. We cannot skip grades in spiritual development."[6]

James Fowler relies on the theories of Piaget, Erikson and Kohlberg as he outlines stages of faith that people may reach as they mature. His definition of faith as a universal human experience is not identical to the classical Christian notion of saving trust in a personal God and divine revelation; it is more akin to how we defined the term *paradigm*:

> Faith is not always religious in its content or context . . . Faith is a person's or group's way of moving into the force field of life. It is our way of finding coherence in and giving meaning to the multiple forces and relations that make up our lives. Faith is a person's way of seeing him - or herself in relation to others against a background of shared meaning and purpose.[7]

The first formal stage of faith development, *Intuitive-Projective* faith (ages two-seven), employs speech and other symbols to make sense of the world. The emergence of concrete operation thinking paves the way for stage 2, *Mythic-Literal* faith. Stage 3 *Synthetic-Conventional* faith involves an uncritical assumption of one's community's perspective. Older adolescents or young adults often move from stage 3 to 4 as they experience changes like moving out of a parents' home or the questioning of allegiance to the views espoused by authority figures. People embracing *Individuative-Reflective* faith (stage 4) accept responsibility for their own beliefs, ethics and world-view. Faith emerges from within rather than being imposed from the outside. Stage 5 *Conjunctive* faith, rarely experienced in the first half of life seeks to comprehend all sides of an issue while retaining a "commitment to one's own truth tradition."[8]

Stage 6 is characterized by *Universalizing* faith. Embodied by such people as Gandhi, Martin Luther King, Jr., Mother Theresa and Thomas Merton, Stage 6 faith is radical in its transforming power: "The rare persons who may be described by this stage have a special grace that makes them seem more lucid, more simple, and yet somehow more fully human than the rest of us."[9]

With this reference to "a special grace," Fowler hints that his stages of faith cannot be contained within the limits inherent in the secular Modern Psychological Paradigm. He cannot keep God out of his paradigm. A person reaching stage 6 is committed to "justice and love and of selfless passion for a transformed world, a world made over not in *their* images, but in accordance with an intentionality both divine and transcendent."[10] This vision of a transformed world reminds even Fowler of the Jewish-Christian Kingdom of God: "In ways that surely transcend the specificity of Jewish and Christian images of the coming Kingdom, God has disclosed the divine intention to redeem, restore and fulfill all being."[11]

Such hope transforms our appreciation of the nature of our lives. In opposition to the Modern Psychological Paradigm, Fowler affirms that life finds its highest meaning not in personal fulfillment but in service for the good of humanity, which is our *vocation*. Vocation is "the response a person makes with his or her total self to the address of God and to the calling of partnership."[12] He concludes:

> What is the shape of human completion and wholeness? Christian faith, in its classic story and vision, tells us that human fulfillment means to recognize that we are constituted by the address and calling of God and to respond so as to become partners in God's work in the world.[13]

By recovering a sense of God's grace and pointing to the Kingdom of God as a future hope, Fowler stretches the horizons of the Modern Psychological Paradigm beyond the individual's life. And by replacing self-actualization with service in partnership with God as the goal of development, Fowler has demonstrated that psychological stage theories of human journeying are inadequate to describe the reality humans experience. He has come very close to embracing the values of the Goal-Oriented Spiritual Journey Paradigm!

How Goal-Oriented Journeying Compares to the Other Models

As a new model, the Goal-Oriented Spiritual Journey Paradigm offers an original perspective on the issues all spiritual journey models must address. We will briefly compare goal-oriented journeying to the other two models in the areas of focus, horizon, dynamics, progress, and the nature of human journeys.

Focus

The Classical Spiritual Journey Paradigm is *theocentric*, emphasizing the role of God as an active agent in the course of a pilgrim's spiritual ascent towards the ultimate existential union with his or her Redeemer. This ascent is *faith-specific*, meaning that it assumes a personal relationship and acceptance of Jesus Christ as Savior and Lord.

The Modern Psychological Paradigm is *anthropocentric*, emphasizing a human developmental ascent that leads towards self-actualization of the individual. It is not faith-specific. This human journey experience does not depend on God's existence.

The Goal-Oriented Spiritual Journey Paradigm is *theocentric but not faith-specific*. Like the Classical Spiritual Journey Paradigm, the Goal-Oriented Spiritual Journey Paradigm presupposes the existence of a personal God who is revealed in and through Jesus Christ as Lord and Savior. This God creates, directs and provides the visions for the numerous dynamic spiritual journey experiences of attaining task-specific goals within one's earthly life. For the Christian, the pursuit of the journey goal is an explicit means of relating to God in Christ in an intentional manner. God is experienced as preparing, calling, and cooperating with the Christian as he or she journeys towards various task-specific goals.

For the non-Christian, the presence of God in a journey is an expression of common grace. Its existence is veiled and often not even recognized by the journeyer. The Goal-Oriented Spiritual Journey Paradigm maintains that God has earthly goals even for non-believers and that they journey towards such goals even though they are not cognizant of the spiritual source that set their journeys into motion.

Horizon

The Classical Christian spiritual journey begins with the call to ascend to God and ends with the experiencing of a state of union with Him. Its journey horizons are the time of personal commitment to God and heaven. The Modern Psychological journey is bounded by the beginning and ending of physical life in this world. The developmental journey begins at birth and concludes at death.

The Goal-Oriented Spiritual Journey Paradigm shrinks the horizons of the spiritual journey. It contracts the time frame by asserting that *our spiritual lives are composed of many short-term*

123

journeys. Instead of needing a lifetime to complete one journey, each of these individual journeys may take one, five, or ten years to travel from beginning to end. It also, like the Classical Spiritual Journey Paradigm, sees the horizons from an eternal perspective by acknowledging that goal-oriented journeys emerge from eternity past (the predestining plans of God are always considered an aspect of phase one) and collectively prepare the journeyer for entrance into eternity future (this world's journeys serve as phase one experiences for the heavenly journey to come).

Dynamics

The Classical Spiritual Journey Paradigm asserts that divine grace is the essential dynamic that fosters change and progress in a spiritual journey. In contrast, the Modern Psychological Paradigm emphasizes the natural/impersonal maturational process.

The Goal-Oriented Spiritual Journey Paradigm recognizes the role of both divine grace and biological, psychological and social human maturational processes. It sees the two as not in conflict, but rather as complementary forces within the matrices of a person's many spiritual journeys. Although the relationship between these forces is complex, it can be summarized in the following way: human maturational processes help to define and to some extent limit the individual context into which divine grace enters a person's spiritual journey.

Progress

Like its predecessors, the Goal-Oriented Spiritual Journey Paradigm employs stage language to describe the course of spiritual journeys. However, the nature of the progress described by the stage descriptions is different. Both the Classical Spiritual Journey and the Modern Psychological Paradigms use stage language to describe progress made in personal growth. In the language of the Classical Spiritual Journey Paradigm, this growth is related to attaining higher degrees of personal holiness or sanctification. Each stage brings the pilgrim closer to God. The language of the Modern Psychological Paradigm relates to levels of maturational growth, in which the person draws closer to the ideal of self-actualization.

The Goal-Oriented Spiritual Journey Paradigm uses stage language not to denote the progressive attainment of desirable personal attributes or qualities, but instead to describe *the progress made in achieving a task-specific, God-ordained, goal.* A task-specific goal involves calls us to fulfill a vision through learning, healing, or service.

A pastor accepts a task-oriented goal when he/she responds to a call to serve a specific church. A Sunday school teacher accepts a task-specific goal when he/she embraces a call to teach a particular class. A person accepts a task-specific goal when he/she personally owns God's call to serve a specific group of people in a particular way (to minister to unwed mothers, to work in a soup kitchen to feed the poor of the neighborhood, etc.). Another person may embrace a healing related task-specific goal by accepting a journey intended to resolve specific psychological problems. The progress made during such journeys may result in personal growth (both in terms of holiness and self-actualization), but the stages are not specifically related to any sequence of personal maturational growth.

As a result, the Goal-Oriented Spiritual Journey Paradigm offers an individualized assessment of each person's spiritual journeys. Unlike the other two paradigms, whose stages describe the common *content* of experience that everyone encounters as they journey, the Goal-Oriented Paradigm prescribes no specific content; it offers no generic goals (such as holiness or self-actualization) that are to be achieved on the road towards spiritual maturity by all persons. Instead, it offers a description of the spiritual journey *process* (the sequence of experiences necessary to achieve any specific goal-oriented journey), regardless of the goal's specific content.

The Goal-Oriented Spiritual Journey Paradigm judges progress according to the Biblical criteria of *faithfulness* in fulfilling God's will. Faithfulness is defined as the achieving of the specific, and multiple, journey goals provided to us by God during the course of a lifetime, in ways that are in accord with God's righteous character and redemptive purposes within human history. Thus, although the specific goals and journey experiences (the content of the journeys) may differ from person to person, the principle of faithfulness to the journey call remains a constant.

The Classical Spiritual Journey and the Modern Psychological Paradigms view the human journey in a unitary fashion. There is one all-embracing goal toward which a singular, life-long journey heads.

The Goal-Oriented Spiritual Journey Paradigm interprets human existence as the composite of a multiplicity of *distinct but related journeys*. There is not one goal to our singular journey in life, but rather an abundance of goals toward which we journey throughout our time on earth. In the course of our lives, some of the goals are realized, while others are not.

We may experience goal-oriented spiritual journeys in a serialized manner (such as Paul's first, second and third missionary journeys), in which one journey chronologically follows a prior journey. We also may experience our spiritual life as a collection of current spiritual journeys that are independent but related or *linked* to one another. A reflective individual may discover that, at any given moment, he or she is involved in several journeys, all of which are complimentary, but distinct in terms of individual journey goals and the progress being made in fulfilling them.

A Unifying Spiritual Journey Theory

Some people might mistakenly imagine that I am asserting that the Goal-Oriented Spiritual Journey Paradigm should replace the Classical and Modern Psychological Paradigms. This is not the case.

In arguing for a contemporary spiritual journey model, I seek to honor the genuinely positive contributions of the Classical Spiritual Journey and Modern Psychological Paradigms. The Classical Spiritual Journey Paradigm correctly emphasizes that holiness is the ultimate goal of the human journey. Similarly, the developmental perspective of the the Modern Psychological Paradigm as a whole seems to me to be undeniable. The emphasis upon the necessity of fulfilling the will of God by embracing the task-specific goals which God calls us to journey toward, which is at the center of the Goal-Oriented Spiritual Journey Paradigm, also appears to me to be undeniable. Since differing religious paradigms may exist side by side without one completely destroying the other, the real question becomes: is it possible for the perspectives of the three paradigms to be unified into a larger whole?

Psychological Stages as Goal-Oriented Journeys

In regard to the stages of growth outlined by the various schools of thought within the Modern Psychological Paradigm, it is possible to describe each stage as a self-contained redemptive-level goal-oriented spiritual journey. For example, previous stages represent phase one for the stage under consideration, and upon its conclusion (phase four), a new stage - a new goal-oriented journey - is embraced. The goals of the journeys are the psychological tasks that define the essence of the journey, and target groups can often be identified in each stage.

Thus, the psychological and developmental truths embodied in the Modern Psychological Paradigm can be embraced "wholesale" by the Goal-Oriented Spiritual Journey Paradigm, with little modification. Stages represent goal-oriented journeys, and the sequential nature of the developmental quest is simply an affirmation of the principle that goal-oriented journeys are often related to one another in a sequential or linear fashion.

The Classical Journey as a Goal-Oriented Journey

The relationship between the Classical Spiritual Journey Paradigm and the Goal-Oriented Spiritual Journey Paradigm can be described by introducing the concepts of the *micro-journey and macro-journey.*

The Goal-Oriented Spiritual Journey Paradigm shrinks the horizons or time-frame of the spiritual journey as a discrete unit of spiritual experience. In a given lifetime, people experience many journeys of limited duration which are related to one another sequentially (a linear progression from one journey to another). Further, a person can experience more than one journey at a time, with each journey complementing the others. Within phase three of a goal-oriented journey, we can often discern repeating patterns that mimic the overall five phase design of the goal-oriented journey, and we labelled these *micro-journeys.*

127

The concept of a *macro-journey* represents the Goal-Oriented Spiritual Journey Paradigm's recognition that the Bible images the Christian life as a faith journey toward a "better country - a heavenly one" (Hebrews 11:16). The spiritual life does not end with death, but rather continues through death into the eternal realm, in which "we will be with the Lord forever" (1 Thessalonians 4:17). The ultimate goal or destination of the Christian life is the "new heaven and new earth" in which the church is united with Jesus as a bride is wedded to her bridegroom (Revelation 19:6-10; 21:1-4). This is the journey that is so well charted by the three stage Classical Spiritual Journey Paradigm.

The same journey experiences can also be interpreted as a lifelong five phase redemptive-level goal-oriented spiritual journey. Since this particular journey is unique in being lifelong, I label it a macro-journey to distinguish it from its shorter relatives. Hence, the Goal-Oriented Spiritual Journey Paradigm is able to incorporate the wisdom and insights of the Classical Paradigm without distorting or compromising its own perspective.

The purgative stage of the Classical Spiritual Journey Paradigm (stage 1) approximates the Goal-Oriented Paradigm's phases one and two. On a trans-personal level, God prepares us from eternity past for the heavenly journey to which we have been called (Ephesians 1:3-14). On a personal level, New Testament descriptions of converts' pre-Christian "former lives" (phase 1) are often coupled with conversion/repentance references (phase 2) and the goal of the journey is clearly the attainment of holiness (Ephesians 2:1-8; Colossians 1:13-22; 1 Thessalonians 4:3; 1 Timothy 6:11-12; 1 Peter 1:14-16).

Phase three of the Goal-Oriented Spiritual Journey is analogous to stage two of the Classical Spiritual Journey. Cooperating with God and others involves a lifelong progressive growth in holiness, in which virtue is added to virtue in light of the promise of God's assistance and glorious provision (2 Peter 1:3-11).

Phase four of this macro-journey is the transition between stages two and three of the Classical Journey Paradigm, involving the embracing of death and the entry into eternal life. Phase five is the enjoyment of the Christian's inheritance - the perfection of heaven and our resurrection from the dead, and it corresponds to stage three of the Classical journey.

Chapter Notes

Chapter One

[1]Robert E. Webber and Rodney Clapp, People of the Truth (San Francisco: Harper and Row, 1988), pp. 19-20.

[2]James E. Loder, The Transforming Moment (San Francisco: Harper and Row, 1981), pp. 30, 33, 55, 108.

[3]Bruce Larsen, Ask Me to Dance (Waco: Word Books, 1972), p. 27.

[4]Vernard Eller, The Outward Bound (Grand Rapids: William B. Eerdmans Publishing Company, 1980), p. 16.

[5]Regarding the propriety of using the term "cooperation" within the context of service and ministry, see Karl Barth, Church Dogmatics, vol. IV: The Doctrine of Reconciliation, ed. and trans. G.W. Bromiley and T.F. Torrance (Edinburgh: T and T Clark Ltd, 1962), pp. 598-610. Though preferring "service" over "cooperation," Barth still admits that the latter term is not necessarily incorrect:

> We must not conceal, let alone deny or even question, the fact that the true being of the Christian does in its own place and manner have a true, significant and effective part in that history. If Christ lives in him and he in Christ, if this common life is not just the action of Christ but his own action, then, although the Christian is certainly not the subject and in no sense the author of the history of salvation which takes place in the action of Jesus Christ, although he is not himself the reconciler or even the co-reconciler, although he is in no sense an independent promoter of the kingdom of God, yet he certainly has a part in that history as a co-operating subject, and in its own place and manner this part is not merely apparent but real, not is it meaningless or superfluous, but significant and effective. But can and should we really describe him as a co-operating subject? We certainly cannot describe the term as absolutely impossible, and therefore we cannot reject it out of hand. Yet, since it might so easily imply too much, it is as well for us to look around at once for another term which will give its precise meaning. (pp. 599-600)

129

See also Jacob Firet, <u>Dynamics in Pastoring</u> (Grand Rapids: William B. Eerdmans Publishing Co., 1986), pp. 129-134; and James W. Fowler, <u>Faith Development and Pastoral Care, Theology and Pastoral Care</u> Series, ed. Don S. Browning (Philadelphia; Fortress Press, 1987), pp. 49-51, who prefers the word "partnership."

[6]Barth, p. 601.

[7]Alan Jones, <u>Exploring Spiritual Direction</u> (Minneapolis: Seabury Press, 1982), p. 101.

[8]Les L. Steele, <u>On the Way: A Practical Theology of Christian Formation</u> (Grand Rapids: Baker Book House, 1990), p. 129; Lucy Bregman, <u>Through the Landscape of Faith: Christian Life Maps</u> (Philadelphia: The Westminster Press, 1986) pp. 54-56.

Chapter Two

[1]My use in this chapter of the Biblical stories about individual's goal-oriented journeys is based on the value of what has come to be known as *narrative theology*. Les Steele, pp. 15-16, describes this hermeneutical tool:

> Narrative theology generally begins with a view that life is more processive or dynamic than static and is best understood as an unfolding story. This implies that our best understanding of the dynamic relationship between God and people comes through story. Canonical story, faith community story, and life story are three types of narrative useful for theology.

> The first form of narrative is the canonical or biblical story. In doing narrative theology from the Biblical text a literary, wholistic approach is used to interpret Scripture. It is literary in that the portions of Scripture that are narrative in form should be interpreted accordingly and, more broadly, the entire canon of Scripture shhould be seen not as a theological dictionary but as the unfolding story of God's relationship with the world. It is wholistic in that it takes Scripture as a whole, not fragmenting and dissecting it until its unity and internal coherence are lost.

Chapter Three

[1]Vernard Eller, The Outward Bound (Grand Rapids: William B. Eerdmans Publishing Company, 1980), p. 12.

[2]Ibid.

[3]Ian Cundy, "The Church as Community," in Obeying Christ in a Changing World, Vol. 2: The People of God, ed. Ian Cundy (Glasgow: Collins Fountain Books, 1977), p. 33.

[4]Elizabeth O'Connor, Servant Leaders, Servant Structures (Washington, D.C.: The Leadership School, 1991), pp. 21-22.

Chapter Four

[1]Nelson S. T. Thayer, Spirituality and Pastoral Care, Theology and Pastoral Care Series, ed. Don S. Browning (Philadelphia: Fortress Press, 1985), pp. 67-68.

[2]Henri J. M. Nouwen, The Living Reminder (New York: The Seabury Press, 1977), p. 59.

[3]Ibid., p. 72.

[4]Thayer, p. 30.

[5]Kenneth Leech, Soul Friend (San Francisco: Harper and Row, 1980), p. 35.

Chapter Five

[1]Shusaku Endo, A Life of Jesus, trans. Richard A. Schuchert (Rutland, Vermont: Charles E. Tuttle Company, 1978), pp. 99-100.

Chapter Seven

¹C. G. Jung, "Approaching the Unconscious," in Man and His Symbols, ed. C. G. Jung (New York: Dell Publishing, 1964), p. 75.

²C. G. Jung, Modern Man in Search of a Soul, trans. W.S. Dell and Cary F. Baynes (New York: Harvet Books, 1933), pp. 99-109; C. G. Jung, Integration of the Personality, trans. Stanley Dell (New York: Farrar and Rinehart, Inc., 1939), p. 3; C. G. Jung, Analytical Psychology (New York: Vintage Books, 1968), p. 138.

³Erik H. Erikson, Identity and the Life Cycle (New York: W.W. Norton and Company, 1959, 1980), pp. 53-105.

⁴Donald Capps, Life Cycle Theory and Pastoral Care, from the Theology and Pastoral Care Series (Philadelphia: Fortress Press, 1983), pp. 13-14, 37-79.

⁵Morton Kelsey, Companions On The Inner Way (New York: Crossroad Publishing Co., 1983), pp. 177-192; and Discernment: A Study in Ecstacy and Evil (New York: Paulist Press, 1978), pp. 107-115. For an illustration of how contemporary Christian spiritual directors employ Jung's model, see M. Robert Mulholland Jr., Invitation to a Journey: A Road Map for Spiritual Formation (Downers Grove: InterVarsity Press, 1993), pp. 50-56.

⁶Kelsey, Companions, p. 180.

⁷James W. Fowler, Stages of Faith (San Francisco: Harper and Row, Publishers, 1981)p. 4; see pp. 9-15. The implications for pastoral practice of Fowler's stages of faith model are discussed in Fowler's book, Faith Development and Pastoral Care.

⁸Fowler, Stages, pp. 119-186.

⁹Ibid., pp. 200-201.

¹⁰Ibid., p. 201.

[11]Ibid., pp. 209-210.

[12]James W. Fowler, <u>Becoming Adult, Becoming Christian</u> (San Francisco: Harper and Row, 1984), p. 95.

[13]Ibid., p. 92.

To order additional copies of *Endless Possibilities*, complete the information below.

Ship to: (please print)

Name _____

Address _____

City, State, Zip _____

Day Phone _____

E-mail address _____

I/we would like to order:

_____ copies of Endless Possibilities @ $11.95 each $ _____
Postage and Handling @ $1.00 per book $ _____
Nebraska residents add 6.5% tax $ _____

TOTAL AMOUNT ENCLOSED $ _____

Make checks payable to: Spiritual Journey Press
6536 Rockwood Lane
Lincoln, NE 68516-5110

Churches and Study Groups:
Please write for bulk purchase, church
and study group discounts.
If your church or group would like to
host a spiritual journey seminar or retreat,
please contact Dr. Spitzer at
the above address.